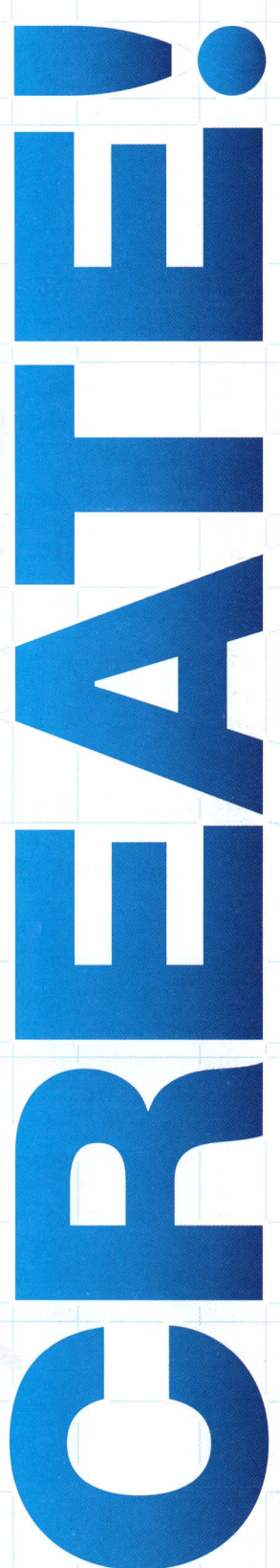

Product Design

Andy Reid
Chris Ralls

Series editor
Jenny Jupe

Heinemann Educational Publishers
Halley Court, Jordan Hill, Oxford OX2 8EJ
Part of Harcourt Education

Heinemann is the registered trademark of Harcourt Education Limited

© Chris Ralls and Andy Reid, 2003

Andy would like to thank Ruth, David and Vickie who started me teaching and to mum and dad for love and support always. Love to Shaena for patience at all times.
Chris would like to say thank you to Crestwood School especially Simon Hall and Richard Wilcock and wife Catriona Ralls for all their help and encouragement.

First published 2003

08 07 06 05 04 03
10 9 8 7 6 5 4 3 2 1

British Library Cataloguing in Publication Data is available from the British Library on request.

ISBN 0 435 41301 5

Copyright notice
All rights reserved. No part of this publication may be reproduced in any form or by any means (including photocopying or storing it in any medium by electronic means and whether or not transiently or incidentally to some other use of this publication) without the written permission of the copyright owner, except in accordance with the provisions of the Copyright, Designs and Patents Act 1988 or under the terms of a licence issued by the Copyright Licensing Agency, 90 Tottenham Court Road, London W1T 4LP. Applications for the copyright owner's written permission should be addressed to the publisher.

Produced and illustrated by Hardlines Ltd.

Original illustrations © Harcourt Education Limited, 2003

Cover design by Matt Buckley

Printed in Italy by Printer Trento S.r.l.

Acknowledgements
The authors and publishers would like to thank Dr Peter Branson for help and advice on the electronic units and Kursty Groves at PDD for valuable information on the design of the Exertris bike.

The publishers would like to thank the following for permission to reproduce photographs: Alamy p. 26 (left and right), p. 54 (left), p. 54 (right), p.68 (top), p. 75 (top), p. 77, p. 78 (top and bottom), p. 82, p. 106 (left); Alessi/Modus p. 96; BBC p. 74; Bubbles p. 49; p. 98; Corbis p. 68 (bottom), p. 79, p. 90 (top right), p. 91 (left), p. 91 (cheese grater), p. 97 (top), p. 106 (right), p. 107, p. 110, p. 111, p. 120; Douglas Annan/Cumulus p. 90 (bottom right); Gareth Boden p.11, p. 12, p. 14, p. 22, p. 28, p. 37 (bottom), p. 38 (left), p. 38 (top right), p. 38 (bottom right), p. 40 (left), p. 40 (right), p. 45, p. 56, p. 57, p. 59 (left and right), p. 62, p. 63, p. 65 (left), p. 65 (bottom right), p. 66, p. 80, p. 81, p. 84, p. 85, p. 85 (top and bottom); p. 94 (top and bottom), p. 95, p. 113, p. 114 (left and right); Haddon Davies p. 104; Hris Honeywell p. 97 (bottom); Imagestate/Alamy p. 37 (top), p. 53 (bottom); PDD Exertris bike p. 50; Peter Gould p. 91 (kettle); Photodisc p. 91 (toothbrush); PhotoObjects p. 61 (top and bottom); p. 65 (top right); p. 91 (chair), p. 111; Robert Harding/Alamy p. 89; Seymour and Powell/Michael Fair p. 90 (top and bottom left); SPL p. 36, p. 53 (top), p. 55, p. 56, p. 75 (bottom), p. 100; Trevor Clifford p. 20 and p. 21.

Every effort has been made to contact copyright holders of material reproduced in this book. Any omissions will be rectified in subsequent printings if notice is given to the publishers.

There are links to relevant web sites in this book. In order to ensure that the links are up-to-date, that the links work, and that the sites are not inadvertently linked to sites that could be considered offensive, we have made the links available on the Heinemann website at www.heinemann.co.uk/hotlinks. When you access the site, the express code is **3015P**.

Key Stage 3 Strategy links
The following logos are used throughout this book to highlight different Key Stage 3 Strategy links.

- (DMA) Design and Make Assignment
- (D) Designing
- (FPT) Focused Practical Task
- (ICT) ICT
- (ABC) Literacy
- (123) Numeracy
- (PA) Product analysis
- (TS) Thinking skills

Contents

Unit 1 — Building on learning from Key Stage 2
Welcome to Product Design! ... 4

Unit 2 — Understanding materials
Introducing metals ... 6
Introducing wood ... 8
Introducing plastics ... 10
Hold on! ... 12

Unit 3 — Designing and making for yourself
Coming up with an idea ... 14
Developing your creature feature ... 16
Making your creature feature ... 18

Unit 4 — Using control to control a display unit
Point-of-sale displays ... 20
Mechanisms ... 22
Electrical components ... 24
Structures ... 26
Materials for a point-of-sale display ... 28
Cuba Tropicana! ... 30

Unit 5 — Exploring materials
Exploring metals ... 32
Finishing metals ... 34
Exploring woods ... 36
Finishing woods ... 38
Exploring plastics ... 40
Finishing plastics ... 42
Product analysis ... 44
Hanging on ... 46

Unit 6 — Designing for clients
Designing techniques ... 48
Design company: a case study ... 50
CAD/CAM ... 52
One-off production ... 54
Designing using electronics ... 56
Spot on! ... 58

Unit 7 — Using control for security
Exploring control systems ... 60
Control systems ... 62
Levers ... 64
Mechanical components ... 66
A bug's life–design brief ... 68
A bug's life–programming ... 70
A bug's life–assembly ... 72

Unit 8 — Producing batches
Manufacturing with MDF ... 74
Risk assessment ... 76
Batch production ... 78
Jigs and templates ... 80
Why pencils are yellow! ... 82
The Entertainer ... 84

Unit 9 — Selecting materials
Smart materials and the environment ... 86
Product analysis: razors ... 88
Design classics ... 90
Product concept model– a case study ... 92
Razor sharp ... 94

Unit 10 — Designing for markets
Designing for consumers ... 96
Market research ... 98
Quality assurance ... 100
Flow charts ... 102
Production for profit ... 104
Just-in-time production ... 106
Light my fire! ... 108

Unit 11 — Using control for electronic monitoring
Introducing radios ... 110
Your circuit board ... 112
Testing circuit boards ... 114
Printed circuit boards ... 116
Design and make a radio ... 118
Designing your radio ... 120

Unit 12 — Moving on to Key Stage 4
Getting ready for Key Stage 4 ... 122

Glossary ... 124
Index ... 127

UNIT 1 Building on learning from Key Stage 2

Welcome to Product Design!

Objectives

In this lesson you will:
- find out about Product Design at Key Stage 3
- learn about the different tools and equipment you will be using in Product Design.

Key words

materials the items different products are made from

equipment the tools used to make the materials into products

Design and Technology is a subject that allows you to be creative and encourages you to develop new skills and knowledge through practical activities. You are about to embark on a series of projects that will develop the skills and knowledge you have acquired during Key Stage 2. With the guidance of your teacher, you will design and make products that people need. Different teachers will help you to learn new skills using some new **materials** and **equipment**.

In this book you will undertake a series of new and exciting projects to solve problems, which will enable you to become more confident in your approach to designing and produce high quality products of which you will be proud. You will learn about many aspects of resistant materials and electronic products and learn:

- what the properties of materials are and how to apply this understanding when designing
- how to select appropriate materials for your ideas
- how to design effectively
- how designers think and create new product ideas
- how ICT can be used in your design work
- how computer-aided design (CAD) and computer-aided manufacture (CAM) are used in industry and how you can use them to produce high-quality products for yourself and others

- about the importance of clear, positive communication
- how quality products are made through effective planning
- how to make products in quantity
- information about manufacturing processes and techniques used in industry
- how to work successfully in a team and the importance of teamwork in manufacturing
- safe working procedures
- how a basic electronic circuit works in everyday objects and how to use this knowledge to help create your own products
- about the use of mechanisms in control systems

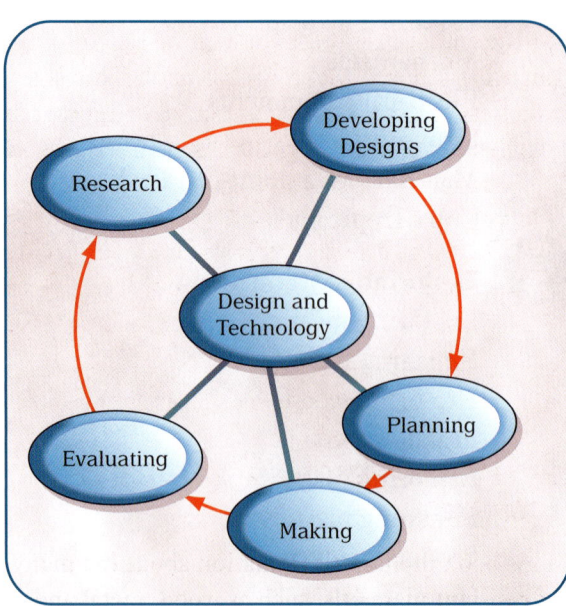

In Design and Technology you will carry out Focused Practical Tasks (FPTs), which help you to learn new practical skills. In Product Design, a Focused Practical Task might include:

- how to use new equipment and tools such as a CAD CAM machine
- how to carry out different processes, for example to create jigs and templates using a pillar drill

- how to work with different materials
- how to use specialist computer programs to design and make products.

Product Analysis

You will also carry out Product Analysis tasks. Here you will evaluate different products and find out:

- who they are designed for
- how they work
- what they are made from
- how they have been designed
- how they have been made.

Carrying out such tasks helps to build up your knowledge and skills and will help you demonstrate your design and technology capability when you carry out Design and Make Assignments.

Design and Make Assignments

At the end of each unit you will be asked to carry out a Design and Make Assignment. This is a practical project which asks you to bring together all the knowledge and skills that you have learned.

The Focused Practical Tasks, Product Analysis Tasks and Design and Make Assignments you carry out in all the different material areas are linked together, so that things you learn in one project will also help you in other projects. You will need to transfer skills from one area to another to become capable.

Product Design materials, tools and equipment

This book includes information about the many types of resistant materials, such as wood, metal and plastic, that you will be working with during Key Stage 3.

There are many different tools and equipment in the Product Design room. The illustrations in B show some of the different things you will use during Key Stage 3.

Think about it!

1. **TS** Think of a product you made at Key Stage 2 in Design and Technology. Try to remember what you did when designing and making this product.

2. **ABC** In pairs, groups or as a class, describe the different products you made during Key Stage 2.

3. **ABC** Name one of the products you made in Key Stage 2 using resistant materials. Write down the following:
   a) Who did you make the product for?
   b) What tools and equipment did you use to make the product?
   c) What things did you like most about the product you made?

4. **TS** Look at the illustrations of product design tools and equipment shown in B.
   a) Which tools and equipment do you recognize?
   b) Which ones have you used before?
   c) What did you use them for?
   d) Which ones will you need to learn how to use?

5. **ABC** Produce a table showing:
   - which tools and equipment you have used before
   - what you used them for
   - how well you used them
   - how easy or difficult they were to use.

6. **ABC** Produce a list of 'dos' and 'do nots' on how to use product design tools and equipment safely.

7. With a partner, spend two minutes talking about which aspects of product design you are looking forward to learning about and why.

Plenary

This book will guide you through Years 7, 8 and 9. Each chapter builds upon what you learned in the previous one, so that when you reach the end of Year 9 you will have the knowledge and capability to proceed to Key Stage 4 with confidence.

UNIT 2 Understanding materials

Introducing metals

Objectives

In this lesson you will:
- find out the useful properties of metals
- find out how some metals behave
- classify metals by their properties and sources
- explore metals by cutting and heating.

Key words

ferrous	a material that contains iron
steel	a hard metal
aluminium	a light silver coloured metal
conductive	a material that can carry electricity or heat
ductile	a material that is able to be shaped and moulded

Product Design is about solving problems and coming up with solutions by using different skills and materials. In this section you will develop an understanding of the properties of materials. You will apply this understanding when designing with resistant materials. At the end of the section, you will make a folder in which to carry your project work for the next three years. This short introductory project is useful to help you become familiar with materials which may be new to you. It may reinforce things you have already found out. It will also introduce you to materials and processes to solve new problems.

Metals

Metal is a relatively modern, naturally occurring material which, when converted into the common forms found today, is probably the most important engineering material of all. Without metal we would not be driving around in cars or flying in aeroplanes. Metals come in three basic types or categories: **ferrous,** non ferrous and alloys. There are many different metals look at the table opposite to see the properties of different types of metals. The two metals that you need to be familiar with are **steel** and **aluminium**.

Metal	Properties	Metal	Properties
Aluminium	Malleable (can be squashed and pushed/bent into shape); polishes up with a little effort	Mild steel	**Conductive**; rusts without treatment; tough and durable (lasts a long time); can be braised and welded; can be cut by hand
Copper	Ductile (can be pulled into a thin wire/shape); conductive	Stainless steel	Hard to cut and drill; non magnetic; glossy
Brass	Polishes up very well; casts with ease; can be used in ornamental objects	Silver	Very expensive and precious metal with high value placed upon it; polishes beautifully; used for small decorative items; lasts a long time
Tin	Used for alloying (mixing) with other metals to change their properties; soft metal that can easily be shaped by hand	Gold	Precious metal with wonderful lustrous yellow shade; high density (heavy)
Lead	Very soft metal; can be shaped by hand; low melting temperature; can be melted and cast in the class-room at low temperatures	Wrought iron	Will not rust; soft metal that can be shaped with a little force and heat treatment

Understanding materials

The use of specific metals in applications is a deliberate decision and by using your knowledge of physical properties of metals, it is possible to see how suitable they are for certain products. For example a jeweller might choose silver or gold for fine jewellery for their lustre. Silver and gold catches and reflects the light around them very well, making them suitable for fine jewellery. However, their expense and relatively low melting point would make them unsuitable for saucepans or kettles. Mild steel is relatively easy to shape using suitable machinery and thus car body panels or frames for chairs and tables are often made from it. However tubes of mild steel would be unsuitable to carry water around a house as mild steel will quickly oxidise and rust away.

Accuracy and measuring challenge

Cutting and shaping metals by hand requires patience and care over detail. Your teacher will prepare a sample of mild steel or aluminium by marking three holes. Your challenge is to try and drill the holes accurately so they line up with each other, paying particular attention to the centre of the holes. You must also file the sides square so that each corner rests at 90 degrees. This is a test of how accurate you can cut and shape. Test your work, and your classmate's work, with a steel rule and a try square.

Circular challenge

Draw a circle on the surface of a sample of mild steel and then score it onto the surface by using some dividers. Now try and cut around the circle using a coping saw, rotating the steel as you journey around the circumference. The saw should always be cutting in a downward motion.

The skill is to cut a perfect circle with minimum filing afterwards. Draw the circle on a sheet of paper to check your accuracy.

Think about it!

1. **TS** Look at B which shows products from the classroom and around the home. Working in pairs, look at each product and discuss what you think about:
   - the way it was made
   - how it works
   - what properties the materials from which it is made must have.
2. Use table A to work out which metals would be used to produce:
   - a kettle
   - a piece of jewellery
   - a commemorative (collectors') coin
   - a food can
   - a sink
   - a table frame or a frame for a chair
   - a car body
   - a large statue
   - picture frame for a wedding gift

B

Plenary

How many metals can you name that will rust and that will not rust? Why do metals rust?

Understanding materials

Introducing wood

Objectives

In this lesson you will:
- find out about the properties of wood
- find out about how different woods behave
- classify woods by their properties and sources
- explore woods by cutting and shaping.

Key words

hardwood	wood from deciduous trees
softwood	wood from coniferous trees
coniferous	trees that do not lose their leaves in winter
deciduous	trees that lose their leaves in winter
man-made board	materials such as plywood or MDF

A

Wood is one of the most commonly used materials known to man. It can be broadly divided into two types: **hardwood** and **softwood**.

Softwood

Softwood comes from **coniferous** trees. Another word for coniferous is evergreen. Evergreen trees do not loose their leaves in winter. In most cases, they have needles instead of broad leaves. Because they retain their leaves all year, they grow quickly and as a result can be grown in large quantities, thus making them economically cheaper to produce and use than other timbers. Softwood is light in colour and can be easily stained. It is easy to work with and shape with the right tools and can be attractively finished. Softwoods found in your school workshop may include Douglas fir, spruce, cedar, Columbian pine, Pirana pine. Picture A shows a coniferous tree and a pine chair.

Hardwood

Hardwood comes from **deciduous** trees, which lose their leaves in winter. Deciduous trees grow more slowly than coniferous trees, this is because they lose their leaves in winter and so in effect stop growing for that period of time. This usually makes hardwood more expensive than softwood. As hardwoods have a close grain structure, they can be cut into detailed shapes without splintering or splitting. Hardwoods are commonly used for decorative furniture as the knots and grains can be made to look very attractive. They are also used in shipbuilding and have been used extensively in buildings over the years.

Hardwoods found in your workshop may include mahogany, oak, iroko, beech, hickory, tulip, ash and sycamore. Picture B shows a deciduous tree and a mahogany cupboard.

Understanding materials

B

🧩 Jigsaw

Design a small jigsaw that is made of simple geometric pieces with a few curves. Using hardwood, softwood and **man-made board** (such as plywood or MDF). Cut out your jigsaws. Which wood is easier to cut? Is it a hard or a soft wood? How does cutting wood differ from cutting metal? Make sure that you file the edges of the pieces carefully so they fit together snugly.

Think about it!

1. Find several different pieces of softwood. Explain the direction and pattern of the grains.
2. Find five examples of products that are made from pine and list them.
3. Find out:
   - why the grain of a door goes from top to bottom, rather than from side to side
   - why the grain of a table goes along its length rather than across its width.
4. Find three examples of hardwoods, Draw them, paying attention to the detail and spacing of the grain.
5. a) Find five examples of products made from hardwood and list them.
   b) Why has hardwood been used instead of softwood for these products?
6. For each of the following items of furniture, state what type of wood is the most suitable choice and give a reason for that application:
   - a chest of drawers for a state bedroom
   - a set of shelves for a kitchen
   - a set of shelves for a garage or classroom
   - a music box or jewellery box
   - a toy box
   - a video cabinet for a living room.
7. When you are working with wood, the fibrous nature of the timber will make a mess. What are the safety or health issues here? How can you manage your working area when cutting wood in the classroom?
8. Find an object in the classroom or from home made from wood that is assembled using a range of joints, for example a frame / storage box, cupboard or shelves. Analyse why the joints in the structure have been used and what forces would be acting on them at different times. Can you suggest other joints that would be more suitable? How would the joints be made?

C

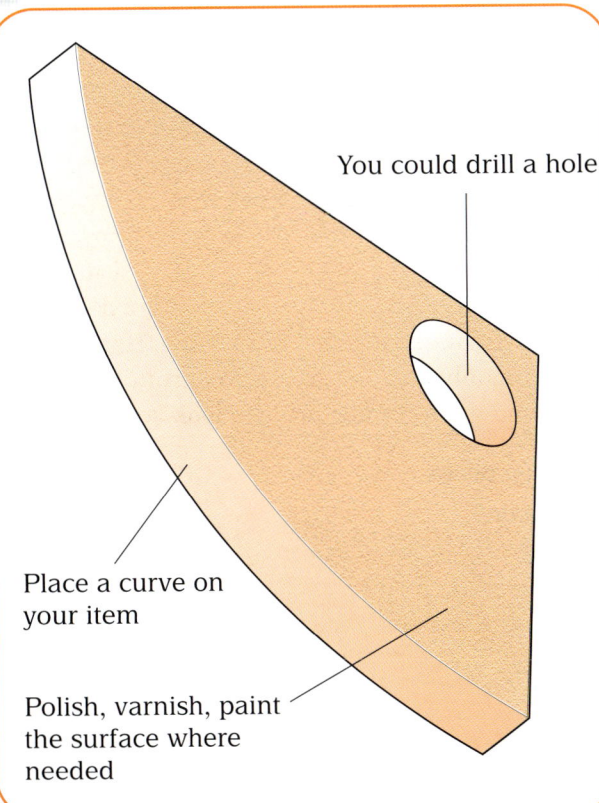

You could drill a hole

Place a curve on your item

Polish, varnish, paint the surface where needed

Understanding materials

Introducing plastics

Objectives

In this lesson you will:
- find out about the properties of plastics
- explore plastics by forming, cutting and heating.

Key words

thermosetting	a type of plastic, that once set, cannot change shape
thermoplastics	a type of plastic that, when resoftened under heat, can have its shape changed many times
PVC	a type of plastic that comes in hard or soft varieties

Thermosetting and thermoplastics

Thermosetting plastics are those plastics which, once set, cannot be re-shaped with the application of heat. They will simply burn. Examples of thermosetting plastic are melamine formaldehyde (desk top covering) and urea formaldehyde (plugs and sockets).

Thermoplastics can be shaped time and time again when heated and they retain their new shape when cooled. Examples of thermoplastics include acrylic, polypropylene (school chairs), and polystyrene (Compact Disk covers) (A). **PVC** or Poly Vinyl Chloride comes in hard and soft varieties. It can be used as house guttering, hose pipes or even clothing.

Using plastics

Forming, cutting and heating plastics are all ways to change the shape of a plastic. A coping saw can be used to cut plastic in curves or intricate shapes. See how many turns you can cut into a piece of acrylic with a coping saw by placing a sample in a vice, working side to side and using the cutting blade back and forth. The acrylic can be cut into detailed shapes this way. For straight lines, it is possible to score along the top surface of acrylic with a cutting

FPT Making a mobile

The aim of this FPT is to manufacture a range of mobiles made from plastics for display in the classroom. In this task you need to use the information you have been given and work in groups. You will need to:
- make sure each component of the mobile is a three-sided shape (you can curve the sides if you wish)
- use plastics
- experiment with as many cutting and shaping techniques as you can.

Equipment:
Scribe
Scalpel
Line bender
Coping saw
Tenon saw
Finishing papers
Files
Steel rule
Center punch
Pillar drill
Wire

knife and then snap the acrylic quickly so that it fractures along the scored line. This will leave a straight edge, but take care as it will be razor sharp. Other plastics, such as polystyrene sheet can easily be cut using scissors. In this way, plastics are often versatile materials for projects.

Heating plastic can also help you change its shape. Acrylic sheet can be heated in an oven for a few minutes and then twisted into new shapes. Placing the new shape into cold water will quickly 'set' the new shape permanently. Careful planning is required however as this is often the last process performed as the plastic will then be difficult to cut, drill and smooth down because of its new intricate shape.

Squashing when heated onto patterns and formers of different sizes can also form plastics. Plastic sheet can also be vacuum formed and moulded into new shapes in a vacuum-forming machine. This machine takes air from under a heated sheet of polystyrene so that the outside air pressure pushes the plastic down over a pattern. The sheet, when cooled, will hold its shape, much in the same way as a jelly mould may look.

Exploring plastics

Take a small piece of acrylic around 200mm x 200mm and cut around the outside and inside using a coping saw. To limit the chances of the acrylic cracking use a sharp drill and work through the small sizes of the drill first, gradually increasing the drills diameter each time.

Using a file, wire wool, emery paper and 'wet and dry' paper polish the edges and internal surfaces of the acrylic. Finally use either an oven or an element strip heater to bend the acrylic into a form that could hold letters or postcards or stationary on a desk. You could even twist it into a shape.

Try slotting together pieces of acrylic and make a four piece 3D puzzle for someone.

Think about it!

1. Find examples of the following plastics: acrylic, polystyrene, PVC, polythene. Stick these samples onto a sheet of paper to include in your file.
2. a) What do the initials PVC stand for?
   b) What is the main ingredient of a plastic?
   c) What was the first plastic called? (A clue – the word begins with the letter B.) Go to www.heinemann.co.uk/hotlinks and click on this unit to find a weblink to get you started with you research.

Plenary

How many times have you picked up an object without thinking what material it is made from or how the surface finish has been produced? Explain how materials you find in the classroom have been processed.

Understanding materials

Hold on!

Objectives

In this lesson you will make a folder, choosing appropriate materials for the job.

Key words

specification a list of criteria that a new design must meet

Think about it!

1. **PA** Look at the ring binders, document wallets, fabric folios and other folders that are shown in A. Carry out a product analysis of these items by answering the following questions.
   a) What types of material have been used?
   b) How suitable is the material for the job?
   c) What could break or wear over time?
   d) Is the surface finish suitable for each folder's purpose?
   e) Is the colour appropriate?
   f) How does the folio keep the work clean and safe from the weather and rough handling?

2. **ABC** Now you have completed your product analysis, write up a five-point **specification** that your folder will have to meet. Think about the following issues when arriving at the specification.
   - What the folio is likely to hold.
   - Who is going to use it.
   - How long it needs to last.
   - What happens to it after its useful life is over.

A

You are going to make a folder to put all of your future design and technology work in. The folder will have to be made to the specification below, follow the drawings step by step to help you.

Equipment

Thick card
Fabric
Samples of wood, metal and plastic
Scissors
Craft knife
PVA, Araldite, Contact adhesive
A4 white card
Pens
Parcel or sticky tape

 **Project folder**

The design brief

With your knowledge of materials you are going to make a folder that will hold your project work for the next three years. The decoration of your folder must reflect what the subject is about and be attractive and informative.

Design specification

- The folder must protect your work from the weather.
- The folder should contain a clip to prevent your papers falling out.
- The folder needs to be made to a high standard within the number of weeks specified by your teacher. This is called a time constraint.
- The information displayed on the outside of the folder needs to cover all the aspects of Design and Technology (including Food and Textiles).

Understanding materials

Step one

Using thick card cut out these shapes to the exact sizes and stick them together using sticky tape.

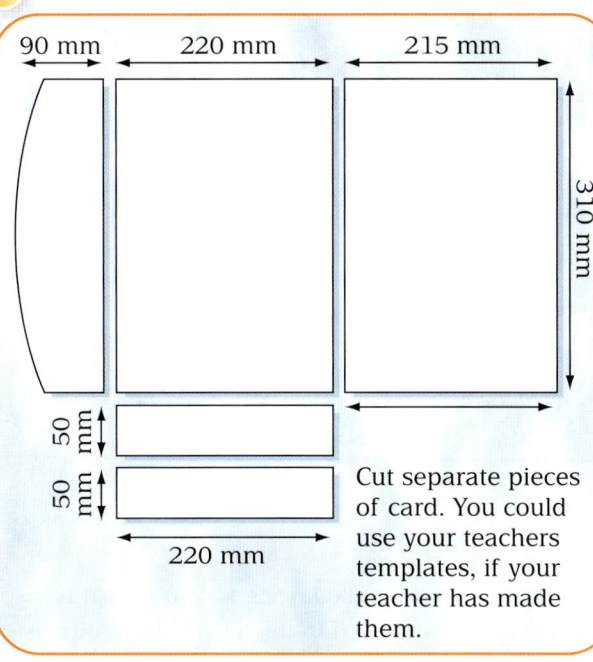

Cut separate pieces of card. You could use your teachers templates, if your teacher has made them.

Step two

Cover your folder using a fabric of your choice. Use an old shirt or pair of jeans, an old pillow case or sweatshirt. Use Copydex or PVA glue.

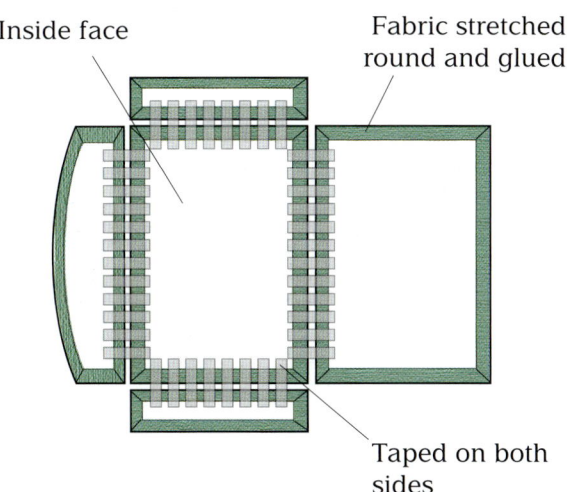

Inside face

Fabric stretched round and glued

Taped on both sides

Step three

Now add a collage of materials to the outside. Use thin examples of wood, metal and plastic, use a contact adhesive such as PVA, Araldite or Evo stick to stick it together.

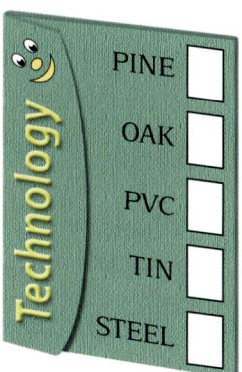

Step four

On the inside stick a piece of blank card to use as a word bank. When you find a new word write it in your word bank and add the meaning next to it.

Investigate a way to hold the folder together, explore existing devices or invent your own.

Plenary

Think about where the materials you have used to make your folder have come from and what you will do with your folder once it can no longer be used. As a designer you will need to find new ways and resources to create the products we use. How will environmental issues influence the way you will live in the future?

UNIT 3 — Designing and making for yourself

Coming up with an idea

Objectives

In this lesson you will:
- learn how to explore ideas and analyze products
- find out what a designer needs to think about when designing and making
- produce a design specification.

Key words

mood board — a starting point for a design idea; a collection of images and ideas that convey a mood or reaction – sometimes known as a mind mapping page

DMA Creature feature

Design brief

A wooden peg is a commonly used product that has been designed to fasten clothes to a washing line (A). However, it has some interesting features which can make it useful as part of another product. Look at the product examples in B to help you design and make a 'creature feature', which can hold notepaper and a pen or pencil.

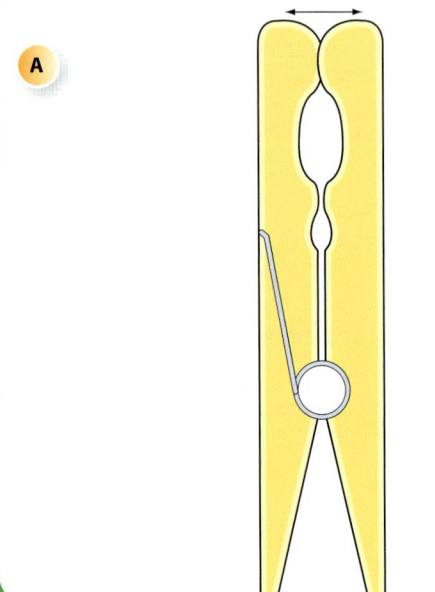

Product analysis

To help you create a good design of your own it is often useful to start by looking at similar products. All professional designers do this, as it is a good way of sorting out what makes a design successful or unsuccessful.

The aim of product analysis is to find out as much about a product as possible. You can do this by taking the product apart, either by looking closely at it or by physically disassembling it. Analyzing a product also involves asking many questions beginning with these key words: how? what? where? when? who? why? This is sometimes known as the 5WH rule. Look at the following example:

How is it made? How does it work?

What is it designed to do? What are the good /bad features? What materials are used?

Why is it that shape? Why has a particular material been used?

Where would it be used?

When would it be used?

Who is it designed for?

By analyzing a product you can begin to understand much more about what the designer needs to achieve through the product. This leads back to the specification, which is a list of attributes that a product must meet.

Design specification

A design specification is a list of the features, that are important in the design of the product. Look at this example for a child's toy.

My toy design should:

- look attractive
- be interesting to use
- be made from easily available materials
- be safe to use
- be easy to make.

Getting ideas

You will also find it useful to collect images of animals or 'creatures' so that you have something to look at for inspiration when you start designing. Most product designers use **mood boards** and often cover whole walls with related images of the things they are designing.

Think about it!

 Write the design specification for your 'creature feature'.

Emotive design

Use the following words to help you come up with images and designs that might help you design your 'creature feature'. Think of how a creature may behave and how it might react to different things:

Creatures may behave:

angry, passive, aggressive, afraid, scared, scary, harmless or dangerous

They may appear:

soft, warm, cuddly, spiky, slippery, smooth, jagged, rough, hard, cool, hot or cold

These words may inspire different colours and shapes and from that mood board of images, you could be inspired to form the shape of your final creature. Mood boards are really important in allowing designers to get ideas onto paper for others to see. Our minds work in very visual ways rather than in a sequence order like lists of words or numbers. At all times we are inspired and influenced by many things and it need only be one small idea in a busy page that is eventually developed into a final design.

FPT Idea creation

Practice and develop your design skills by redesigning existing products. With a friend alternatively say out loud the first word that comes into your head in response to the words that they say. This kind of technique is called free association and is used to tap into the creative side of the mind without realising. It is possible to come up with more ideas and more creative solutions using this technique. You will develop this skill later, but for now see if you can design the following – no matter how bizarre!

Draw the smell of an orange

Design soft

Sketch happy and sad

Free word associate with each other and start with these words, after six goes stop and sketch the thing you have said.

beach   cord   smoothie   craggs   spikes   magic

Think about it!

1. **PA ABC** Look at the range of peg products in B and discuss them with another person. Jot down as many things as you can about the products by using the 5WH rule. You might find it easier to draw a spider diagram or mind map when doing this. The answers you come up with reflect the design criteria that were set out when the product was designed and made.
2. **TS** What is the purpose of the features on a wooden peg?

Plenary

Get used to doodling and experimenting with colours and textures by producing mood boards to help you with your designs. Often the first thoughts you have are the best ones, so get them down on paper quickly and develop them.

Designing and making for yourself

Developing your creature feature

Objectives

In this lesson you will:
- develop your idea by producing a detailed drawing
- use techniques of sketching, rendering and annotating your design
- modify existing ideas.

Key words

rendering	adding colour, form or texture to a drawn or made object
annotating	notes on a design that explain the materials used and how it will work
evaluated	thinking about why and how products are designed and made and how they function
isometric	a way of drawing objects in three dimensions

Designing

Now that you have written a specification for your 'creature feature' you need to produce a range of ideas to develop. This requires a number of skills:

- thinking
- **rendering**
- **annotating**
- sketching.

Thinking

This is made easier when you have some visuals, such as a mood board, to consider. Mood boards influence design and can help you design in order to reflect the mood of the board you have created. You should look at each part of your specification and try to satisfy each part. For example, the feature of attractiveness means considering ideas on colour, shapes and sizes. Try to break the designing job down into small parts and tackle each problem individually.

Rendering

Rendering means adding some colour or variation in line thickness to a sketch to give an impression of what the product might be made from or to make it look lively and interesting. Look at the three simple tips in A and try to apply them to you own ideas.

Annotating

Annotating involves adding notes about your designs which relate to your specification. The annotations only need to be a few words long but should give information about the design, such as how it might be joined together. They also give reasons why a design is very successful or less successful. Annotations should always provide extra information – do not just state the obvious!

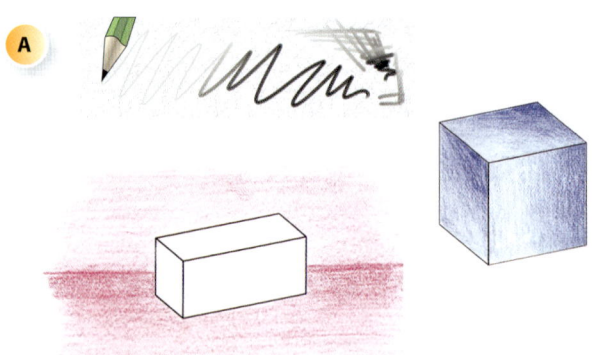

A

Sketching

Sketching means putting ideas down on paper freehand, without the aid of a ruler. Ideas can be quite rough and unrefined at this stage. Do not worry about making each idea look neat; the aim is to get ideas down quickly so that they can be **evaluated** and then developed into more detailed ideas later. As a guide, consider the following.

- Sketch quickly using a soft pencil, such as 2B.
- Use **isometric** underlay to help draw in 3D.
- Produce a range of ideas.

Designing and making for yourself

- Sketch individual parts as well as whole concepts.
- Do not reject an idea just because it may not look as good as others.

Redesign

Take an existing product such as a chair or a watch and redesign it in a style of range that already exists such as Alessi.

The famous designer Alec Issigonis who designed the original sketches for the minicar did so on a dinner napkin. Designers such as Philippe Starck, Michael Marriott, Pier Castiglioni and Jane Atfield have all made use of existing objects to design their famous pieces.

Developing an idea

Once you have a range of ideas, you can make a decision as to which you want to develop into a final idea. It may be that you like a number of features from a few of your initial designs; if so, try combining these together and see what happens.

When developing an idea, you need to refine it and add more detail. Ask the following questions about your design. If you can satisfy each one then you are ready to begin making it.

- Do I know what size my design will be?
- Do I know what each part will be made from?
- Do I know how each part will fit together?
- Do I know how to make each part?

Think about it!

It is important that you practise the drawing techniques that you have looked at here. Draw six boxes on a sheet of A4 plain paper and do the following tasks, one in each box:

a) make a box look like a piece of wood
b) make a box have a reflective surface
c) imagine the box is 6mm thick, write the overall dimensions inside the box
d) draw a clothes peg and label the parts neatly
e) sketch a cube and show tone on its sides
f) draw a circle and make it look like a sphere.

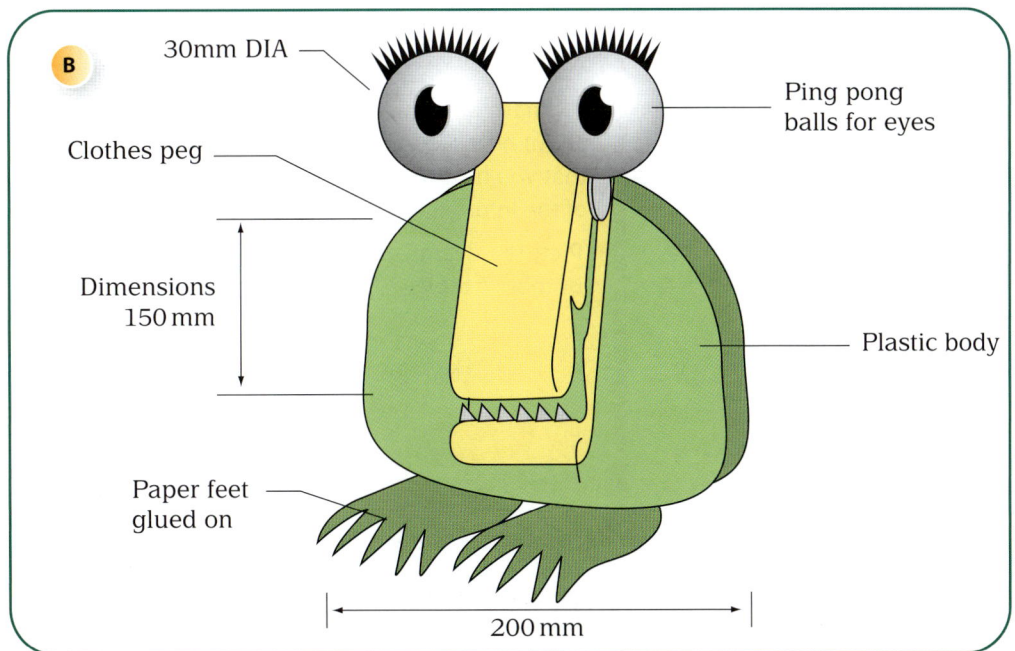

Include a parts list for all the items you will be making and also include any fixings like screws, nuts or washers.

Produce a detailed drawing of your chosen design with all the details included so that someone else can understand how to make it (B).

Plenary

Remember, sketching an idea is only half the exercise. It is just as important to label your design so anyone can understand your ideas.

Designing and making for yourself

Making your creature feature

Objectives

In this lesson you will:
- model your idea to help you finalise you design
- use a range of cutting, shaping and forming processes
- investigate different holding devices
- use appropriate hand tools to cut and form materials safely.

Key words

jig	a device manufactured to assist designers and makers to maintain accuracy when repeating the same operation time and again
pilot hole	a small hole used to guide a screw
aperture	a gap, or shape cut within a material
soft jaws	jaws of a vice that will not damage the surface of a material

Modelling your creature feature

Before you begin to make your creature feature it is a good idea to create a model of the idea. Modelling an idea does not need to involve card or foam or require you to recreate the parts from other materials. An idea of how the creature feature could look can be reached through experimenting using existing products, shapes, components and or reclaimed materials. For example, by using ping-pong balls for eyes, a lemonade bottle for a body, or rulers and pencils for arms and legs, you can quickly but imaginatively use materials to create the feel for your product.

To make your creature feature you will need the following:

- a drawing of your design
- a cutting list for all parts
- jigs and templates to help cut out each part and ensure quality.

You will also need to know how to mark out, cut, shape and finish the materials.

Marking out

For good quality making you should check that the material being used is prepared accurately – cut square, flat and without any obvious defects. You will then need to mark out your materials accurately.

Cutting and shaping

A variety of hand tools can be used to cut out your 'creature feature'. When using any cutting tool you must take care to learn how to stand properly, hold the tool correctly and ensure that your work is clamped.

Holding your work

Holding work in a vice, clamp or **jig** is important as it leaves you with two hands free and gives the work a firm support. You can be sure that the work will not move when you are sawing, filing or sanding the work.

Think about it!

You have been using new tools and learning about new processes. To help you remember all that you have learned, create a table to look at all of the information at a glance.

Picture of tool	Name of tool	What it is used for	How it is used	Health and safety
	Hacksaw	Cut metal	Hold work in vice and saw	Keep fingers away from saw stroke

Think about it!

Make a model for your creature feature. Remember that you do not have to use the same materials that you will use for the final product.

Why do you think it is important to make a model of a prototype?

Designing and making for yourself

Tool	Uses
Marking tools	
Pencil	Never be without a pencil; keep it sharp for accurate scribing.
Steel rule	These have accurate divisions in millimetres. Note that zero is right on the end of the rule, unlike a plastic ruler.
Try square	Used for marking a line at right angles to an edge.
Marking knife	Used for scoring a line across the grain of wood to help when cutting with a saw. Go over the scored line with a pencil afterwards.
Marking gauge	Used to help mark depths along an edge of wood. It is quite difficult to use and will need a bit of practice.
Bradawl	Used to mark the centre of a hole in wood and to act as a **pilot hole** for a wood screw. *Used to mark the pilot hole position on adjoining piece of wood.*
Templates	You will probably be familiar with these being used to mark out a shape onto a work piece. Use card and a sharp pencil to ensure accuracy.
Cutting and shaping tools	
Tenon saw	Used for cutting straight lines in joints. They should be used with a bench hook.
Coping saw	Used for cutting curves in thin wood or sheet material such as plywood. The blade can be adjusted to cut in different directions. It can also be removed and put through a hole to cut out an **aperture**. *plastic/wood; coping saw blades face backwards; vice; use scrap wood to protect your work*
Holding tools	
Bench vice	There are two basic types: wood worker's vice with wooden jaws and metal worker's vice with hard steel jaws. You can use the metal vices if a set of **soft jaws** is fitted.
G-clamps	Useful for clamping work flat to the bench or for clamping two pieces together when they have been glued. *Accurate positioning; Pre-drilled metal block (jig); G-clamp holding jig into poition*
Jig	A jig is a tool which helps you to perform a task more easily by holding piece of work while you drill it or when part of your design is awkward to hold or clamp. Your teacher will be able to help you with this.

A *Tools and their uses*

UNIT 4 Using control to control a display unit

Point-of-sale displays

Objectives

In this lesson you will:
- learn product marketing at the point-of-sale
- consider different approaches used to market products
- identify the important features of communication for marketing, including movement
- classify motion into four kinds.

Key words

point-of-sale display	a device to promote new products
endorse	to give approval to a product
reciprocating	movement backwards and forwards in a straight line
rotary	circular movement
oscillating	movement back and forth along an arc
linear	movement in one direction only

without falling over. You may have seen them in high street shop windows or in the foyer of a cinema or theatre or at a fairground.

You have probably noticed that on a successful point-of-sale display:

- the product/idea/service or offer is always named
- the manufacturer is always mentioned
- there is a range of bright colours
- there is usually a slogan
- sometimes a celebrity is used to **endorse** the product
- there may be an enlarged image of the actual product.

In this unit you will solve small control problems using different materials and techniques. By using a point-of-sale display as a basis you will build mechanisms and electronic circuits that could be used on a point-of-sale display.

Point-of-sale displays (POSDs)

Point-of-sale displays are devices used to promote new products, ideas or opportunities. They carry information on them about the new product being sold and when the product will be released. They attract attention through the use of colour, sound, movement, light and text. They are made of card similar to photo mount board and arrive in flat pack format with a set of instructions for assembling them. They are free standing (requiring no supports) and have been designed to withstand the occasional knock

An example of a point-of-sale display used in a shop to promote products

Using control to control a display unit

Attention can be drawn to a display through the use of flashing lights or moving parts. In moving POSDs, there are four main categories of movement. These are:

- **reciprocating** – movement backwards and forwards in a straight line
- **rotary** – circular movement
- **oscillating** – movement back and forth along an arc
- **linear** – movement in one direction only.

Is this a good point-of-sale display?

Think about it!

1. What do you think makes a good point-of-sale display?

2. a) **ICT** In groups, use a digital camera to collect five examples of point-of-sale displays from your local area.
   b) Present your display to the class explaining:
   - what the products are
   - where they were found
   - what colours were used
   - what sizes they were
   - what you liked about them and why
   - what you disliked about them and why.

3. **TS** Think about a children's playground in your local area and the sort of apparatus found there.
   a) For each item of apparatus and each activity listed below, identify the types of motion:
   Swings, see-saw, roundabout, slide, tyres on ropes, rocking horse, children on a climbing frame, children running around in the park, kite flying.
   b) Can you identify any other types of motion in the playground?

Think about it!

D Using your designing skills produce a card design model for a POSD that will promote a new adventure playground for the school. The POSD will go in the foyer of the school and feature all the apparatus that the playground will have. In pairs, you will need to identify the motions in the playground and then work out how they could fit onto the POSD. For example, the see-saw (oscillating motion) could be achieved by cutting a strip of card to act as the see-saw and using a paper fastener to hold it in position on the POSD board.

Plenary

TS Now that you know the different types of motion, try to mimic each type of motion using only your bodies. In pairs, mime one of the playground activities and see if the class can identify:

a) what the activity is
b) which type of movement you are using.

21

Using control to control a display unit

Mechanisms

Objectives

In this lesson you will:
- describe mechanisms that can be used to change one kind of motion into another
- use pulleys to solve lifting problems
- recognize and understand the purpose of simple mechanical control elements such as CAMs, gears and pulleys.

Key words

cams	objects that sit on a crank and bring about a change in motion
gears	meshing wheels with teeth that link together to transfer motion
pulleys	a series of wheels connected by ropes or belts and used to transfer or lift loads with little effort
eccentric cams	off-centered wheels on a shaft
bevel gears	toothed gears that are set at an angle
fulcrum	pivot point
pivot	point around which an object turns

Mechanisms that can change one type of motion into another type of motion include **cams, gears** and **pulleys**.

Cams

Cams are found in car engines, steam engines and small toys. The example in (A) is an **eccentric cam**. Cams are often pear-shaped in appearance and are used to change rotary motion into reciprocating motion. They cannot work the other way round, as they are not necessarily fixed to the cam follower all the time. Cams can also be used to transfer rotary motion in a horizontal plane to rotary motion in a vertical plane.

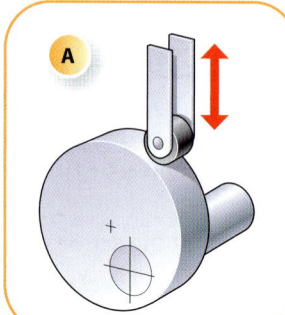

Gears

These are circular objects with teeth around the outside which are designed to reduce the effort within a system or transfer power and motion from one place to another. Gears can be found in wind-up clocks, old machinery, lawn mowers, bridges, cranes, and bicycles (B).

C An example of a bevel gear can be seen in this hand held drill

Bevel gears are similar to gears because they have teeth, which work together; the main difference is that the teeth are cone shaped instead of cylinder shaped. Bevel gears are used to change rotary motion in a horizontal plane to rotary motion in a vertical plane or visa versa.

A good example of bevel gears working in this way can be found on a hand drill or wheel brace (C). When turned the large bevel gear attached to the handle produces an increase in the amount of turns from the small bevel gear attached to the drill chuck.

Pulleys and pulley systems

Pulleys are round discs that can support rubber belts, rope, or chain. This allows motion to travel greater distances across a mechanism with less components being used.

Pulley systems use a combination of pulley wheels to rescue the effort used to lift or move a load. A good example of a pulley system can be found on yachts, where a heavy sail can be winched up by one person and lifted into position a little at a time (D).

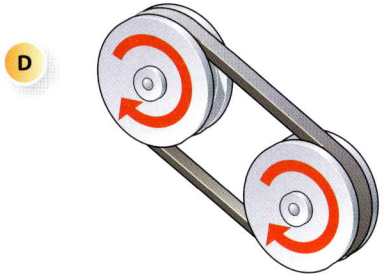

D

Linkages

Linkages are used to control movement and change the direction of a force. They can also make things move at the same time, or move parallel to each other. Linkages often do several of these things at any one time. Linkages such as bell cranks can be used to change the direction of force round a corner.

Linkages can be used to change the distance moved, by moving the **fulcrum** or **pivot** along its length. You will find linkages in windscreen wipers, deckchairs, collapsible pushchairs, bike brakes and ironing boards.

FPT Working mechanisms

See if you can link all four of these mechanisms in one frame so that one turning handle rotates the whole system.
- A cam and follower
- Three gears in a gear chain
- A pulley belt
- A crank and crank shaft

Use Pro/Desktop to create a 'virtual model' of a mechanism system and see it work for real. It is also possible to save each image of the mechanism as it rotates and import those images into PowerPoint or a similar presentation package. Those images can be run continuously and as a result you can produce a movie sequence of the mechanism you have created.

Think about it!

Now that you know how mechanisms work, you can solve the pulley lifting problems shown here. Work in pairs or small groups.

1. On a sheet of A4 paper draw several circles (pulleys) of different sizes using coins or a compass.
2. Number the pulleys randomly from one to twenty.
3. a) Ask your partner or group members to join up the pulleys with a single line (one long imaginary rope) so that when number one is turned in a clockwise direction it will ultimately lift a load that is attached to the other end of the rope around pulley number twenty.
   b) Which way does pulley number twenty turn?
   c) Can you make the tasks harder by disguising the pulleys and making the distances to cover both smaller and larger?
4. TS A heavy load needs to be loaded onto a ship. You need to use six pulley wheels and one length of rope to move the load effectively and carefully.

   Hint: use your Internet search engine to look up mechanical advantage or go to www.heinemann.co.uk/hotlinks and click on this unit. This may help you solve the problem.

Think about it!

1. TS Working in small groups, list examples of cams, gears and pulleys. Discuss the advantages and disadvantages of each system such as:
   - wear and tear
   - expense
   - ease of use
   - maintenance of system.

Plenary

Make a list of everyday objects that use cam gears and pulleys. Can you imagine what life would be like without the use of them?

Using control to control a display unit

Electrical components

Objectives

In this lesson you will:
- construct a simple electrical control circuit
- recognize and understand the purpose of simple electrical control elements such as switches, buzzers, resistors and LEDs
- see how you can use electrical components to create movement in a point-of-sale display.

Key words

electrical components	small devices that transfer electric current into other forms of energy or change electric current flow
insulator	a material that blocks electricity or heat
resistance	materials that resist electric current and turn it into heat
Light Emitting Diodes (LEDs)	a small bulb used in a electric circuit
switches	a break in the circuit that can be controlled safely
buzzers	a component that vibrates when a current passes through

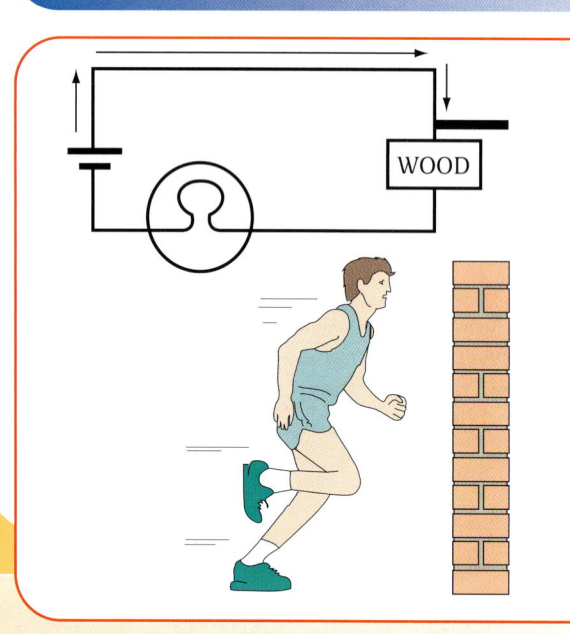

In order to understand how to use **electrical components** to improve your POSD, it is important to understand a little about how circuits and components work.

An electrical circuit allows electricity to flow through materials a bit like an athlete running around a race-track. Electricity cannot flow through electrical **insulators** (just as an athlete cannot run through a wall). Electrical wire is surrounded by a layer of insulating plastic (PVC). The material inside the plastic (the wire) allows electricity to flow. By connecting wires from one place to another, it is possible to make components light up, move or buzz.

You will encounter many new words when working with electricity and electronic circuits for example voltage, **resistance**, conduction and short circuits. Voltage or volts are units of electromotive force or electric potential. A small battery has a potential of 1.5 volts. The square shaped battery you might use in your lessons has a potential of nine volts. A plug socket in your house will have 240 volts connected to it and an overhead pylon cable may contain 765,000 volts. Resistance is needed in a circuit to control the voltage from the battery. Resistance is obtained by using a resistor. A small **Light Emitting Diode** or LED does not require the full nine volts to make it illuminate, it only needs a small amount of it. A resistor is used to reduce the voltage and safely light the LED. Any material that allows electricity to pass through it is said to be conductive, conduction is where electricity is allowed to pass through a material. A short circuit is a term used to describe an electrical current that does not follow a correct path because it has found a short cut. This short cut may be the result of poor soldering, touching wires or a component being wrongly connected or positioned.

Power supplies

Use batteries when making or testing circuits, four to nine volts can be used in nearly all small electrical circuits found in point-of-sale displays. Small lights (bulbs or LEDs) can be powered effectively this way. Do not connect your ideas to the mains supply!

 Conduction test

Use a nine volt cell, two crocodile clips, some wire and a light bulb to test different materials to see whether they conduct electricity or not. Record your results on a table and place them in your file for future use.

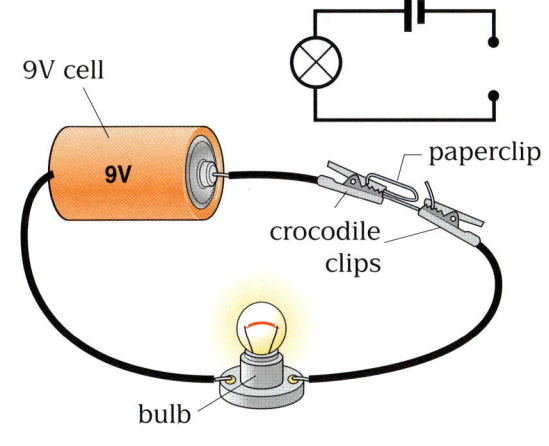

Materials to test:

Wire	Cotton
Wood	Nylon
Paper clip	Tin foil

Drinks can	Watch strap
Pair of scissors	Pipe cleaner
School tie	Cocktail stick

Electrical components

Electrical components are small devices that transfer electric current into other forms of energy or change electric current flow. You could use these in your display along with a mechanism. The following components can be used to create effective circuits:

- switches
- buzzers
- resistors
- LEDs.

These are all likely to be powered from a battery source.

Switches are breaks in the circuit that you can control safely. These are used in your home to turn lights on and off, and to control the stereo or television. They are usually made of an insulating material (plastic) to keep you safe.

Buzzers are components that vibrate when a current passes through them. They will make a sound as the electrical energy is changed into movement energy making a small part of the device vibrate very quickly. Buzzers could be switched on and off as moving parts of your display pass over each other.

Light Emitting Diodes (LEDs) are an effective way of creating lights that attract attention in a point-of-sale display. They connect in one direction as current can flow through in one way only.

Think about it!

1. **TS** Think about your own house. Where is a buzzer used? What is it used for and for how long does it buzz?
2. Where are LEDs found at home or in school? What colours are used and work well?

Plenary

Test yourself! In pairs, take turns to explain what is meant by

- conduction,
- insulation,
- current,
- voltage,
- resistance
- short circuit.

Using control to control a display unit

Structures

Objectives

In this lesson you will:
- learn about different types of structures
- build robust structures designed to support weight
- evaluate structures made by your class
- consider effective and ineffective designs.

Key words

structure	the way something is put together
compression	a squashing force
tension	a pulling apart force

A point-of-sale display is a form of **structure**. Structures are found in the natural world and in everyday objects. It is possible to recognize patterns found in nature that have been replicated by engineers and architects (see A). For example, think about the correlation between:

- spiders' webs and electricity pylons
- an egg and the Millenium Dome roof
- a bee honeycomb and the Eden Project conservatory in Cornwall.

These structures involve ties and struts, which are the names given to beams and supports that are subject to differing forces of stress and strain.

Forces

Compressive force is a squashing force. For example, when you are sitting in a chair, the legs of the chair are under **compression**. When an orange is squeezed over an orange squeezer, a compressive force is exerted.

The force in **tension** is a pulling apart force. For example, in a tug of war a rope is being pulled from either end. The rope is under tension.

A beehive honey comb

The Eden Project building

Using control to control a display unit

A building is a mixture of complex structures

Making a structure

There are a number of terms that are used to design and make a structure. These include:

- strut – a beam used in a structure that is under a compressive (squashing) force
- tie – a beam in a structure that is under a tensioning (pulling) force
- span – a distance between two points in a structure
- beam – a part of a structure that carries a load
- shell structure – a self supporting canopy.

It is important that you become familiar with these terms to help design your own structures.

Think about it!

1. **TS** Working in pairs, create three free standing structures from card that will support this textbook 150mm off the desktop. Do not use glue!
2. Carry out a test to explore which of the three structures best supports this load.
3. **ABC** Describe what characteristics of the design and the construction made it the most effective.
4. Give your three structures to another group for evaluation. Identify the forces and stresses within the structures you have been given. Report back to the groups.

Plenary

The next time you visit a workshop, look at the many structures and supports used in its construction. Look at the ceiling space and try to work out where the weight has been dispersed.

Using control to control a display unit

Materials for a point-of-sale display

Objectives

In this lesson you will:
- build on your materials knowledge and understanding
- concentrate more on modelling with materials
- consider which materials you will use to construct your point-of-sale display.

Key words

correflute	corrugated plastic sheeting
foam board	foam sandwiched between card
corrugated card	two sheets of card sandwiching a corrugated core
mounting board	thick card
MDF	man made fibre
PVA glue	water-based adhesive

Materials

Each material listed below is made in a different way, but they share one common property; they can all be printed on. This might be worth remembering when designing your point-of-sale display.

- **Correflute** is corrugated plastic sheeting.
- **Foam board** is a layer of foam sandwiched between a layer of thick card.
- **Corrugated card** can be found in the form of cardboard boxes.
- **Mounting board** is thick card that is stiff and smooth. It is often used in picture frames and photographs to give a professional finish.
- **MDF** is the shortened name for medium density fibreboard and is a man-made timber. It comes available in a range of thicknesses.

Examples of materials: corrugated card, plastics, MDF

Adhesives

All glues need the application of pressure when joining two pieces of material together. Here are some adhesives that could be used in your point-of-sale display:

- **PVA glue** is a water-based adhesive which can be applied to one or both surfaces that are to be joined. The materials being glued need to be water permeable. When pressure is applied the glue is forced into the fibres of the material where it sets and thus grips the two surfaces together.
- Stick glue, such as Pritt Stick, works in the same way as PVA but it is less messy and dries more quickly. However, it cannot hold onto great weights.
- Hot melt glue works by melting a solid plastic onto two surfaces which, when cool, forms a bond that hold the two pieces together. The melted plastic holds onto the fibres on the surface of the material rather than soaking into it. It is an ideal glue for joining dissimilar materials together.
- Double-sided tape is used as a quick non-messy method of holding lightweight materials together. It is ideal for laying paper sheets on top of each other. It is useful for point-of-sale displays as it can be included in the flat pack and used in conjunction with the assembly instructions.

FPT Materials database

On an A3 sheet of paper, cut out and stick down as many different types of materials as you can find. Label each one. Describe it and state whether you think it could be used in a POSD. This will form part of a useful materials database later.

Think about it!

1. Carry out a test using the following adhesives: PVA, stick glue, hot melt glue and double-sided tape. For each one note down the following:
   - drying time
   - ease of use
   - degree of messiness
   - waste produced
   - preparation time
   - cost
   - appearance once dry
   - safety issues.

2. Write down the areas on a point-of-sale display where double-sided tape could be used.
3. ABC ICT Design a small instruction leaflet that explains how to use double-sided tape for people who have not used it before.

Plenary

With a partner, identify all the materials and adhesives you have learned about so far. Make sure you know two properties about each material and adhesive.

Using control to control a display unit

Cuba Tropicana!

Objectives
In this lesson you will design a point-of-sale display that uses movement, including simple control, to advertise a holiday resort.

Key words
POSD — a device to promote new products

Designers always need to find new and interesting ways of advertising. Even television adverts, which may be seen as a short film had the original ideas first drawn out on paper. Adverts in magazines and newspapers often take the form of a picture showing the product and a slogan, but some advertising takes a three dimensional form. These forms are often referred to as point–of–sale displays or POSD's and are often seen at your local cinema or video/DVD rental shop. The cardboard cut out of James Bond is not just there to look good! It will have information including the new film title and release date. A good POSD design will attract your attention, maybe by using a flashing light, pictures of explosions or attractive film stars.

Point-of-sale displays are not needed for long periods of time. However, when they are displayed, they are likely to be knocked, handled roughly, touched frequently or exposed to extremes of damp or sunlight. This treatment and the environment affect the condition of the POSD and make an impact on the quality of its appearance.

To help with the planning and manufacture of your POSD do some observational sketches and drawings of existing products. Make notes of the materials used and the techniques that have been applied to hold it together when being used. You might be able to borrow one for your class to use for this.

In small groups you will form a new design agency who specialise in commissions associated with POSD's. Think of a name for your agency and appoint one person as the lead designer who must

DMA Cuba Tropicana!

Cuba Tropicana is a new holiday resort in a far distant land. It is a colourful, vibrant and fashionable place. All the drinks are free and all that is missing is the sea – but you can sunbathe by the pool!

The design brief
Your brief is to advertise the facilities and attractions of this holiday resort on your POSD. The POSD must either have a moving part or attract attention with an electronic circuit or a combination of both.

Design specification
Make sure the project is safe. It needs to be free standing, eye catching, informative, recyclable and easy to construct. The POSD has to be posted for less than £3.50. (This offers a research opportunity at the Post Office.) Include instructions for constructing the POSD.

listen to everyone's ideas before helping to make the final decision.

Use a flip chart or A3 sheet in the centre of the table and create a mind map of all the different aspects of the project including the materials, planning, tools, ideas, movements, safety and production. The design brief is quite specific in some areas, but less so in others and will allow you to be creative and imaginative.

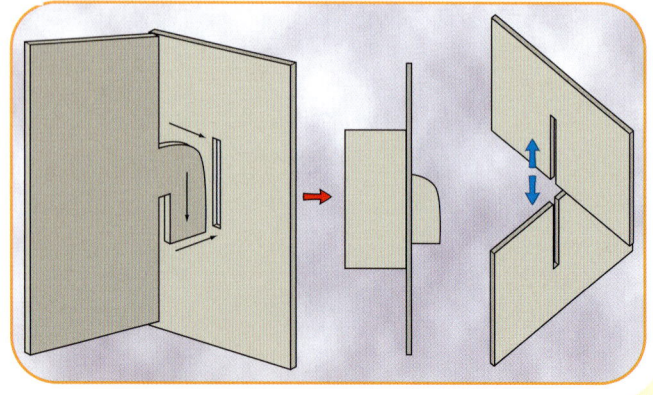

FPT Clips and slots

Practice making the clips and slots from pieces of card. Make a small version of your display from A3 mount board or corrugated cardboard. The display will not have the moving mechanisms or electronics but you will get some idea of the final design of the front and an indication of where the mechanisms will fit and how they will work.

Carry out a product analysis of your design at this stage. Assess how the display looks and how well it will perform.

Try out different types of clips and fastenings to determine what will be the best method of clipping the device together. Is it worth enlarging the clips to match the added weight of the display stand? Remember that a small clip could easily bend and deform under stress.

Designing for other users

You can now negotiate a design specification amongst the class, just as real designers do when designing for other users. Make sure your product is safe, eye catching and makes economic use of materials and resources. The work you carried out during the first part of the course will enable you to recognize the best way to plan and carry out this practical activity and manage your time and materials.

Manufacturing the POSD

You can connect pieces of card and plastic together by building tags and slots into the sides and edges. This will mean that several pieces can slot together. If you look at the illustration in A, you will see that it acts very much like a pizza box or other cardboard packaging. Take care to plan your work first. Remember to build in the tags so you do not have to attach them to the board afterwards.

Think about it!

What adhesives could you use to stick any extras onto your POSD?

How many different types of POSD's can you find? How are they constructed and what do they sell? How has the designer of the POSD got your attention and displayed the product for sale? Look at the different font types used. Has the designer used a font type that corresponds to the mood of the product?

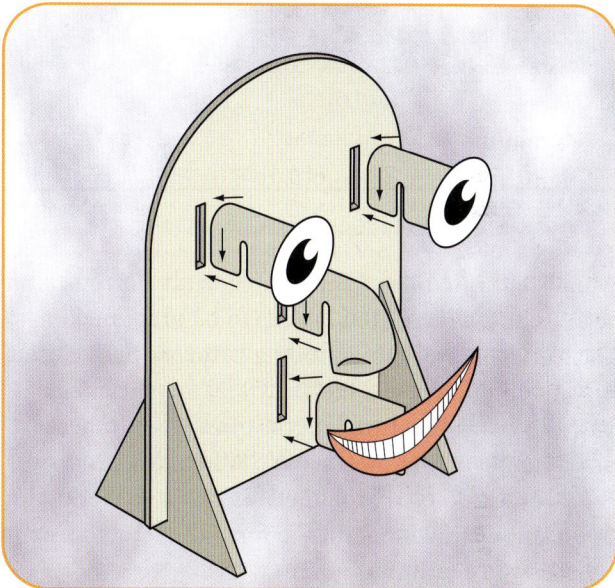

Plenary

Advertising using point-of-sale display has many advantages and disadvantages. Make a list of them and see if they apply to other forms of advertising.

UNIT 5
Exploring materials

Exploring metals

Objectives
In this lesson you will:
- explore more complex properties of metals
- use new tools to cut, shape and form metals
- use CAM to cut and shape metal.

Key words
steel	a hard metal
aluminium	a light metal
planish	to smooth, flatten or finish metal

There are many different types of metals, but the two metals that you will need to be most familiar with are **steel** and **aluminium**. Both are strong, relatively inexpensive metals to purchase and can be shaped and cut with hand tools and joined in a variety of ways. They have a lustre when polished but can also be painted or **planished** to achieve different decorative effects (B).

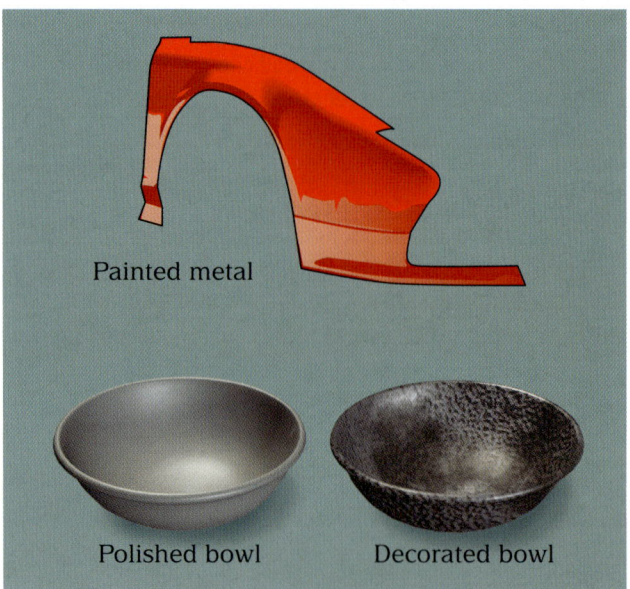

Painted metal

Polished bowl   Decorated bowl

Metals fall into one of three categories – ferrous, non ferrous and alloys. Metal needs to be processed or turned into a workable product before it can be used effectively. When in a molten state, metal can be extruded or rolled into lengths of rod, bar, tube, sheet, angle or channel (see A). When this process has been completed, the metal is easier to work with and can be joined together to form the structures and devices you see and use every day.

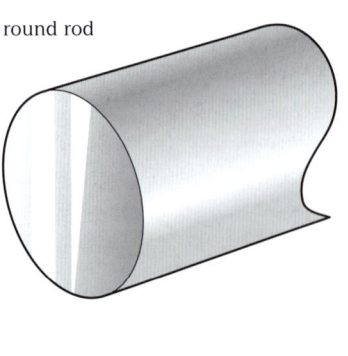
round rod

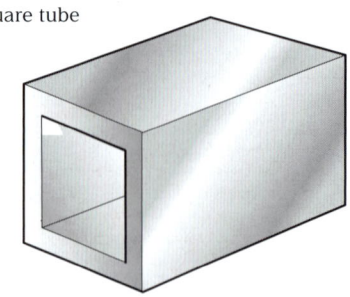
square tube

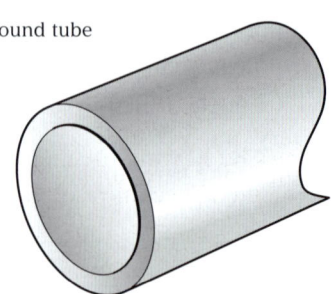
round tube

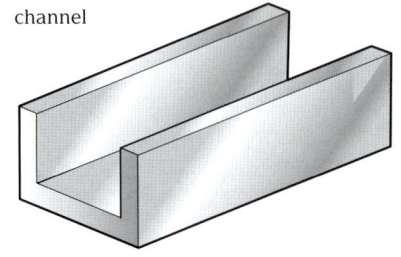
channel

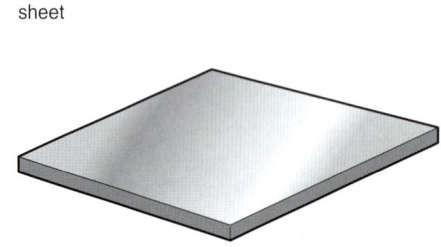
sheet

angle

Changing the physical properties of metals

So far you may have encountered metals in the workshop such as mild steel sheet, duralumin, copper, brass and stainless steel. It is unlikely that silver, gold or platinum are stacked up somewhere! However you can change the physical properties of materials and their aesthetic appearance by adding different elements or exposing metals to high temperatures for specific periods of time.

When two or more metals are mixed together during the smelting process, an alloy is formed. This new metal retains some of the physical characteristics of each of its components and is more versatile as a result.

Common alloys are:

- Brass - a mixture of zinc and copper
- Bronze – a mixture of copper and tin
- Duralumin – a mixture of pure aluminium and a small percentage of copper
- Chrome stainless steel – iron, carbon and chrome

Think about it!

Look up these metals on the Internet and find out the specific percentages of each parent metal in the alloy.

Heat treatment

When you handle and cut and file metals, they become 'work hardened'. Their physical grain structure changes and makes the metal tougher to cut and shape. By heating the metal slightly and cooling slowly the metal becomes softer or 'annealed'. The process of heating and cooling to change the properties of metals is called heat treatment.

Exposing medium carbon steel to a high temperature and then cooling (quenching) it very quickly in water or oil, changes its physical properties making the steel very hard, but also very brittle. By heating the metal up once more to a slightly lower temperature it reduces the brittle properties without losing its hardness.

The 'tempering' of metals in this way allows designers and manufacturers to help find solutions to problems that require metals to behave and perform in specific ways.

Heat treatment

If there is a hearth in your school department, with your teacher, heat some mild steel in a flame until it glows bright orange. The mild steel needs to be square in section approx 10mm along each side.
Allow it to cool slowly. You can twist it into a spiral by slotting it over the top of a bending bar with a 10mm square hole in the center. This allows you to apply the necessary twisting force easily.
Evaluate how easily the metal will do this compared to a piece of non-heated mild steel.
Eventually the mild steel will twist no more and becomes firmer…why do you think this is?

Think about it!

 Find out what the following terms mean
annealing
quenching
soaking
normalising
tempering.

Try and use these words when you are working with materials.

Plenary

Look up heat treatment on the Internet and specifically search for tempering colours. What applications can you find for metal that has been heated until it turns purple?

Finishing metals

Objectives

In this lesson you will:
- explore ways in which metal can be finished
- understand why different metals are finished in specific ways and why.

Key words

lustrous	when an object has a shiny or reflective surface
oxides	a compound of oxygen

Most metals are **lustrous** meaning they shine when light falls on them and this reflects from their surface. The smoother the surface, the more reflection the metal will give and the shinier the metal will appear. Jewellery makes use of this property of metal as do alloy car wheels, chrome additions to car bodies, or furniture, interior decorations or some ornaments and decorative metal sculptures. Lustrous metal suggests quality, expense and rarity.

Sometimes however, metals need to perform more functional roles or have a specific surface finish if they are going to be used in certain applications.

To smooth a metal surface down a file is used to remove any large scratches or indentations. Smaller and finer files are used to smooth down the surface further and emery cloth is used to make final preparations.

'Wet and dry' papers are used for the final preparation of the metal by providing a very smooth surface finish but before any paints can be applied the metal must be degreased using methylated spirits on a rag. Handling the metal by hand leaves grease and moisture on the metal surface. These **oxides** could later accelerate metal corrosion or prevent successful final finishing with paints.

Painting

Before the final layer of paint is applied metals require primers and undercoats. The best results are produced when lots of thin layers of paint are sprayed on to the metal and the surface is rubbed down with 'wet and dry' papers between each coat until its smooth.

Paint does not cover up mistakes. It only makes them more visible! It is always better to invest the time in the painting process rather than rush the task and be disappointed with the end result.

Painting is used for a variety of reasons on metal, particularly to cover large areas and to make things more visible and attractive. Paint comes in many colours and therefore makes choice and variety easy.

Plating

Durable but decorative metals such as silver or chromium can be applied to softer metals such as brass and copper using the plating method. Here the brass or copper is placed in an electrolysis tank along with a sample of silver or chrome. An electrical current is passed between the two and slowly over time, the silver or chrome will cover the brass or copper object as it dissolves and travels through the electrolytic solution. Some cutlery sets give an example of where electrolysis plating has been applied.

Planishing

By physically denting the metal in small 'cup' shapes no bigger than the end of a pencil, an attractive effect can be achieved on soft metals such as aluminium and copper or brass. This effect hardens the metal as it is applied leaving a rigid but eye catching surface finish.

Plastic Dip coating

Here the metal sample is heated and then dipped into a reservoir of fine plastic granules, these can be any colour. The metal will melt the plastic and stay in contact with it until it cools. At this time the metal has a fine coating of plastic that keeps it from corroding. Some furniture and piping make use of plastic coating. Often metal objects that are likely to be knocked around are plastic coated to avoid obvious damage being so visible.

Enamelling

Here a fine ceramic mixture is literally baked onto the metal surface. Ovens are an obvious application where enamelling has been used as the surface needs to be wiped clean for hygienic reason but more obviously withstand the hot internal and external temperatures of an oven.

Think about it!

(TS) How are the metal desk or chair legs of the classroom furniture finished? Why is this? What about objects you find at home? How has a particular metal object there been finished and why?

Finishing experiments

This experiment will not only demonstrate how well certain surface finishes work but will also act as a durability test. Take five samples of mild steel, approximately the size of a playing card.

- Sample 1: spray on a series of paints, undercoat primer and then a gloss surface finish
- Sample 2: rub down in wire wool and emery cloth and then cover in a film of machine oil
- Sample 3: rub down in wire wool and emery paper until it shines and then leave it
- Sample 4: enamel the forth sample
- Sample 5: do nothing to this sample

Drill a hole through the corner of each one and leave in a line outside the workshop and note how their appearances may change over a six-week period.

Which seems to have lasted longer and why?

Surface finishing techniques

Carry out each of the following surface finishing treatments on small samples of mild steel or aluminium. The focus of this task is to experiment with surface finishing techniques and enhance your practical skills knowledge. The samples can then be cut out to make jewellery or badges.

- spraying paint onto the surface
- planishing (using the back of a ball pane hammer and hitting the metal into a firm sand bag)
- plastic coating or enamelling

Plenary

Why is it necessary to have such a wide range of surface finished available to metals?

Where is it appropriate to have a surface planished instead of electroplated?

Exploring woods

Objectives

In this lesson you will:
- explore more complex properties of woods
- use new tools to cut, shape and form woods
- use CAM to cut and shape wood.

Key words

coniferous	trees that do not lose their leaves in winter
kiln	a large oven or furnace for drying

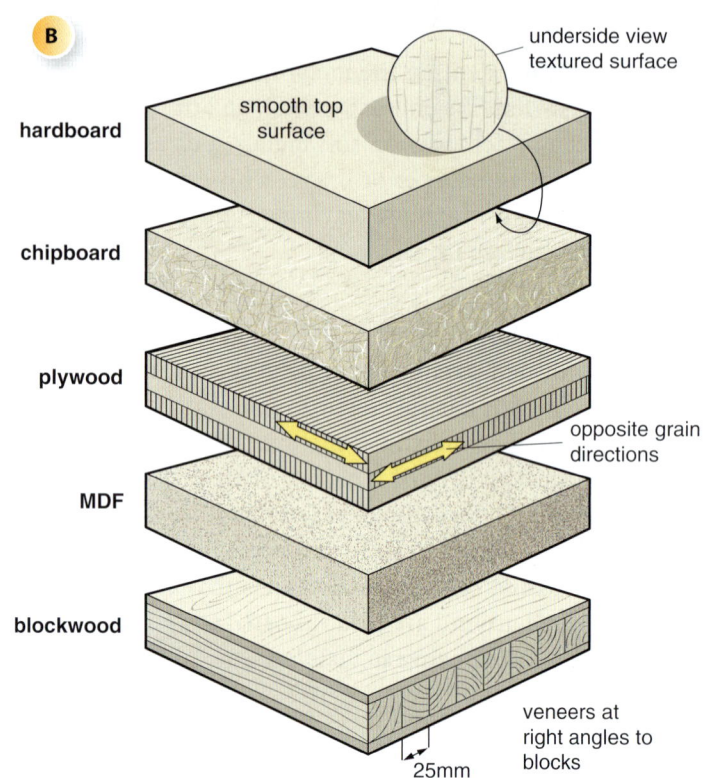

B

Wood

There are two major categories of wood: natural wood and man-made timber. Natural timbers come from either hardwood trees or **coniferous** softwood trees. Man-made timbers are manufactured in sheets that are often much larger than the wood taken from a tree. All timbers have particular characteristics making them suitable for a range of applications (see unit 2, Understanding Materials page 8). It is important that you learn to identify and become familiar with these characteristics, as timber is the most popular material that designers use.

Softwood

There are many woods you could use in your project but you are mostly likely to use pine. Pine is light in colour and can therefore be stained to look like many other different types of wood. Some people like the look of knotty pine. Douglas fir has this quality. It is the cheapest type of pine as it grows quickly and is weaker due to the amount of knots in it. Pine is easy to machine or process as it is softer than hardwood.

A

Pine trees

Hardwood

Hardwoods come in many different colours. The grain patterns differ but generally tend to be tight or close together. This is because the cells are much closer which result in the wood being denser or heavier than softwood. Hardwoods are harder wearing than softwoods and are often more expensive. This is because the processing of hardwoods is more expensive and they are rarer because of the length of time they take to grow.

Teak is a naturally oily hardwood that is very durable, has an attractive grain pattern and is orangey brown in colour. It was a very popular wood in the 1970s where the demand for teak house furniture was huge. As a result of its popularity, teak supplies became scarce and very expensive. Good quality teak, that is with straight grain and a minimal amount of knots, has become very difficult and expensive to purchase.

Exploring materials

C

Oak tree

Seasoning

After a tree has been felled, whether it is a softwood or a hardwood tree, it will be cut up into long, thick planks and left outside, sometimes under cover, to dry out. Using a **kiln** can speed up this process. When wood dries out the cells contract and can put twists and bends into the timber. This needs to occur before the plank is cut down to its finished length, width and thickness. Finished planks that have twists in them will most likely have come from a tree that has not been seasoned properly.

Man-made woods

MDF is a manufactured board. It can come in many thicknesses, usually in large sheets, and is made by mixing fine wood particles and adhesive together. Care must be taken when cutting however as the dust can be harmful.

Plywood is another manufactured board, consisting of an odd number of layers glued together using an adhesive called resoursanal formaldehyde. The different layers are glued at 90 degrees to each other making the timber strong in both directions (D). The more layers the plywood has, the stronger it is, but also the more expensive.

A close up view of the layers of plywood

D

FPT Marking and cutting

123 Cut a piece of timber into two halves, mark and cut along each side to produce two lap joints (see E). Swap with someone else who was working with a different piece of wood and align the two pieces together. To complete this you will need to refine your marking out and cutting skills.

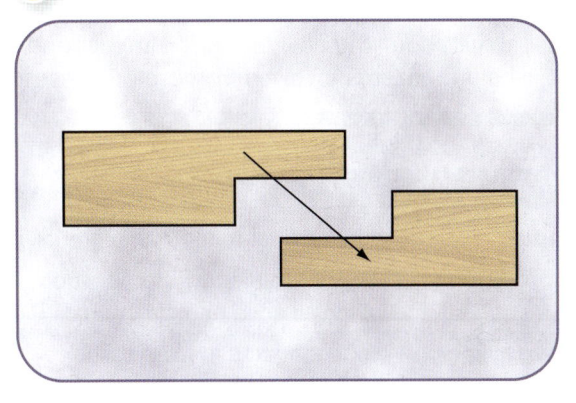

E

File and glass paper the joins so that they line up at 90 degrees to each other and they rest smoothly and level with each other. Glue the two pieces together and wipe away excess adhesive. In doing so try to minimize the amount of glue that gets carried across the surface of the work.

This is a good marking out and cutting exercise and when this is dry it allows you to practice some surface finishes.

Think about it!

1. Working in groups, examine the following items:
   - a lamp
   - telephone
   - computer mouse.
2. For each one, identify:
   - what materials it is made from
   - the suitability of the materials for the function and for safety
   - how the materials have been finished.
3. ABC Choose one of the items and carry out a life cycle analysis by drawing a flow chart to show the materials used from source to disposal.

Exploring materials

Finishing woods

Objectives

In this lesson you will:
- explore ways to finish woods
- understand why different finishes are used and where
- think about the environmental impact and health hazards involved in these processes.

Key words

finish	to put a final coating on material
wood grain	the lines made by fibres in wood which all go in one direction
glasspaper	a paper coated in glass particles used to smooth wood

B

A tenon saw is used to cut a straight line in a piece of wood. Note how the saw is held in the hand and the wood is held in place on the table to increase control

C

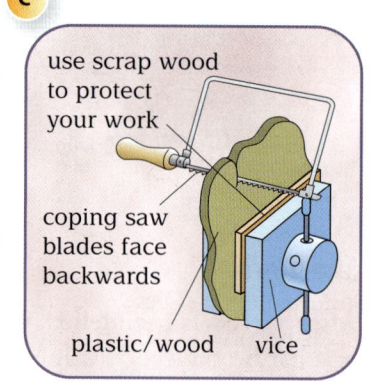

use scrap wood to protect your work
coping saw blades face backwards
plastic/wood   vice

A coping saw can be used to cut a shark bite design. You will gain more control if you ensure the blade is cutting when you pull it towards you. Make sure the teeth are pointing towards the handle

Shaping wood

You learned how to shape wood in unit 2, page 8. In this project, you can put your skills and knowledge into practice and use a combination of tenon saws (B) and coping saws (C) to achieve accurate and intricate shapes. Jack planes (D) and abrasive glass papers (E) will also be used to achieve the smooth **finish**.

D

A jack plane can be used to remove waste wood and to ensure a 90° straight, flat edge to the face of the wood

E

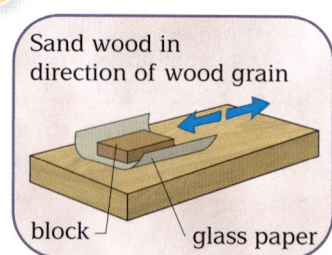

Sand wood in direction of wood grain

block   glass paper

*Sanding improves the appearance and feel of your product. Always sand in the direction of the **wood grain**. Start with a course grit paper and end with a fine grit paper*

Using files and glass paper

Cross filing and drawer filing (F) are used to accurately shape down the surfaces of materials to the correct size. For the final surface finish you can use **glass papers**, emery papers and 'wet and dry' papers which all come in different grit sizes; a small number grit paper denotes a rough texture whereas a large number denotes a finer paper.

A

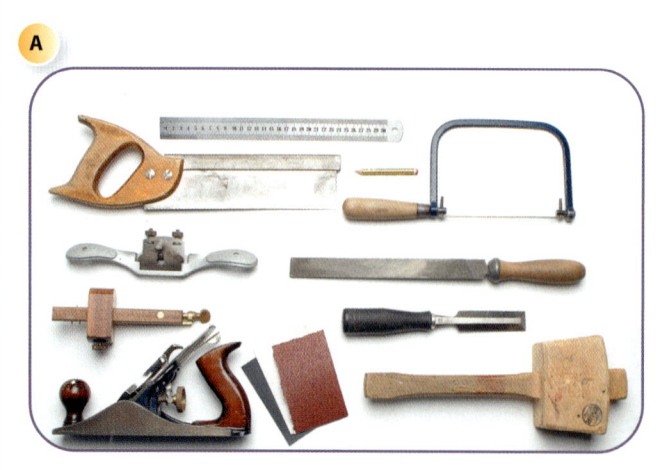

Tools used to shape and measure wood

F

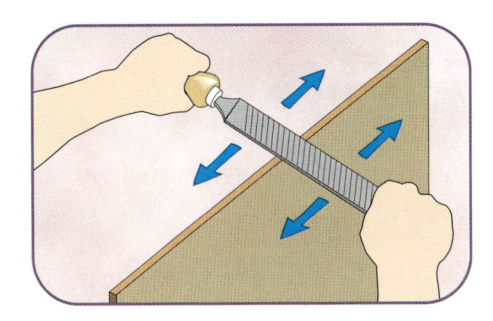

You can work down through the papers to acquire a smooth finish in wood and a shine in metals and plastics. Final polishing and a gloss finish in plastics and metals can be achieved with cream cleaner (such as Autosolve / CIF), running a flame along the edge of plastic, or applying a wax polish and rubbing against a buffing wheel. 'Brasso' cloth and fluid can also be used.

Finishing processes for wood

Once a smooth finish has been obtained, white spirit on a lint-free cloth can be used to rid a wooden surface of grease and dust that may not be visible to the naked eye. A decision on what finish is required then has to be taken. There are many different applications available.

Paint

Paint can be used on wood, metal or plastic. Several thin coats rather than one thick one produce the best results. Gloss (shiny) enamel paint will provide a hard-wearing, cleanable finish. A matt paint produces a slightly duller finish that will not catch the light so readily.

Wood stain or dye

Wood stains and dyes allow colours to be applied while still retaining the natural grain of the wood. The dye is applied with a cloth or brush. Thin strokes produce a rich tint while thick strokes produce a thicker tint.

Varnish

Before any varnish is applied, it is recommended that a 50-50 mix of sanding sealer and varnish is applied to the surface of the wood before the final coating. This 'seals' the wood and ensures a better final surface finish. A polyurethane based varnish essentially applies a plastic coating over the wood that seals in the grain and leaves a wipe-clean, long-lasting and hard-wearing finish. However, the fumes given off are harmful and you should only apply it in a well-ventilated area. Water based varnish is a safe alternative to polyurethane. It is slightly milky when applied but dries more quickly to give a clear finish. Brushes can be cleaned in water.

Think about it!

ABC Look at the tools in A and complete the following table.

	Tool	Use
A		
B		
C		
D		
E		
F		
G		
H		
I		
J		

Finishing

Experiment with each of the surface finishes on the sample that you prepared earlier.

For example you could try wax polish on one side and French polish, staining or varnish on the other.

Make a 'samples collection' as a class to use as reference for the future.

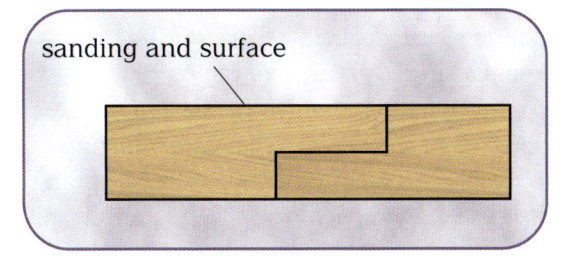

sanding and surface

Plenary

Putting a final finish on a product is a process that must not be rushed. Thin coats should be used to build up layers of finish. What might happen if you try and cover the product you make in one coat?

Exploring materials

Exploring plastics

Objectives

In this lesson you will:
- understand the properties of plastics
- learn about shaping plastics
- understand more about processing plastics, including thermosetting and thermoforming
- understand safety considerations when working with plastics.

Key words

vacuum forming — a process which moulds a thin plastic sheet to form a shape

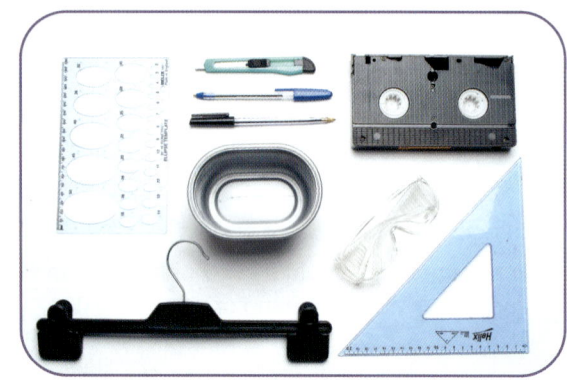

A

Different types of plastic and their uses

There are two major groups of plastics: thermoplastic and thermosetting plastic (see pages 10–11). Thermoplastic is a plastic that can be reshaped with the application of heat which can be done at a low temperature in an oven or **vacuum forming** machine. There are many types of thermoplastic, including polystyrene, polyvinylchloride (PVC), acrylic and polypropelene. Thermosetting plastic is a plastic that once set cannot be reformed with the application of heat. Once it is set and heated again it will simply burn.

You should become familiar with polystyrene and acrylic during this unit. You should also learn how to recognize the major plastics from the products they are made into and the symbols on the side of the products.

In 1988 the Society of the Plastics Industry, inc. (SPI) introduced the resin identification codes at the request of recyclers around the world. Each code represents a different type of plastic. Use the information in table C to help with future work.

Plastic can be shaped using heat. This can be applied over a strip heater, in an oven or using a vacuum former. A vacuum former uses the pressure of the atmosphere to push down soft heated plastic over a pattern to form a mould to the shape you required. A mould is made and placed inside the machine. The plastic is then heated and when sufficiently pliable, the mould is raised into the plastic. The air is then sucked out of the machine, drawing the plastic over the mould. An oven or a strip heater can be used to twist or bend plastics into a variety of curvy shapes that may make your idea more interesting.

B

Polystyrene vacuum forming sheet comes in many colours and varying degrees of thickness. It can be cut using a craft knife, tenon saw or coping saw

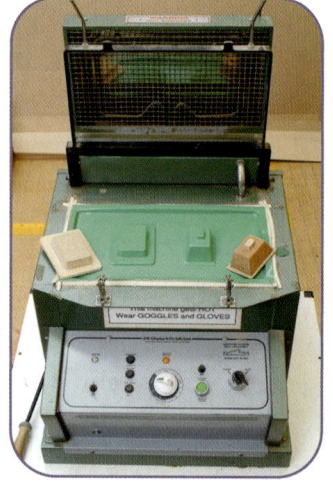

Safety when using plastic and plastic forming machines

When cutting and shaping plastic using hand tools, you need to apply the same considerations as you would when cutting wood. You also need to remember these extra safety precautions.

- Once cut, a plastic edge can be very sharp. Take care not to cut yourself by being aware of the edges.

Code	Description	Properties	Uses
PET (1)	Polyethylene terephthalate (PET or PETE): clear, tough and has good resistance to moisture, heat	Light, sparkling, 'crystal clear' appearance, very tough and durable	Plastic soft drink and water bottles, mouthwash bottles, ovenproof film and ovenproof food trays, duvet filling
HDPE (2)	High-density polyethylene (HDPE): HDPE packaging can be clear or coloured. It has a good resistance to household chemicals	Wide range of colours, stiff, hard, tough, easy to process, cheap, chemical-resistant	Buckets, bowls, milk crates, chemical drums, quality kitchenware, cable insulation, margarine tubs, detergent bottles
V (3) PVC	Vinyl (polyvinyl chloride) or PVC: can be rigid or flexible, extremely resistant to household chemicals	Wide range of colours, durable, weatherproof, strong, resistant to grease and oil	Electrical insulation, plumbing fittings, pipes and gutters, floor coverings, shampoo bottles
LDPE (4)	Low density polyethylene (LPDE): used where heat sealing is necessary. Excellent flexibility and resistant to chemicals	Wide range of colours, soft, durable, waxy, tough at low temperatures, easy to process	Squeezy bottles, toys, lids, wrapping films, carrier bags
PP (5)	Polypropelene (PP): excellent chemical resistance, strong, high melting point	Very tough and durable, resistant to moisture, grease, oil, heat and chemicals	Chairs, hospital equipment, suitcases, hinges, ketchup, yoghurt and margarine containers
PS (6)	Polystyrene (PS): very versatile, can be rigid or foamed, low melting point	Can be hard or soft, good insulator and shock absorber, used in injection moulding	Buoyancy, CD cases, protective packaging, model kits, cups, trays, plates, bottles, pens, coat hangers
OTHER (7)	Other: this code indicates the use of a less common plastic/resin or a combination of different resins	Depends on resin or combination of resin	Three or five gallon reusable water bottles, some ketchup or citrus juice bottles, drawing equipment

C *Table C Resin identification codes*

- Plastic dust remains hard when damp unlike wood dust, so eliminate the risk of getting it near your eyes by wearing goggles.
- Plastic forming machines involve the use of heat. Always receive instructions from your teacher before using them. Remember that heat may travel along the surfaces of the machine as it is made of metal which is a good conductor of heat.
- Never leave a machine unattended as the plastic will melt and there could be a fire.

Plenary

Look at some everyday plastic objects. Can you find the resin code? Look at Table C to see why that plastic has been used for that purpose. Always remember to check you are using the right plastic for the job when designing.

Think about it!

ABC Use the information in Table C and the plastic products in A to complete the following chart.

	Product	Plastic
A		
B		
C		
D		
E		
F		
G		
H		

Exploring materials

Finishing plastics

Objectives

In this lesson you will:
- explore ways to finish plastics in a variety of ways
- understand why different finishes are used and where.

Key words

resin — a solid or liquid compound used in products

As well as using heat to shape plastic from one form to another it is possible to add interest to surfaces made from thermoplastics. Paint and varnish are suitable surface finishes for your products but you can also use stickers and other self-adhesive materials as clean and colourful surface applications. It may be possible to make use of CAM machines in school or a Stika Cutter to produce the surface finish. When processed your design can either be etched onto the surface of a material or peeled off as a self-adhesive sticker.

Heating acrylic plastic, for example up to around 160–170 degrees, allows you to push into the surface metal items such as coins, keys, buttons, and so on. After allowing the plastic to cool, the surface can be smoothed down and then polished with a cloth.

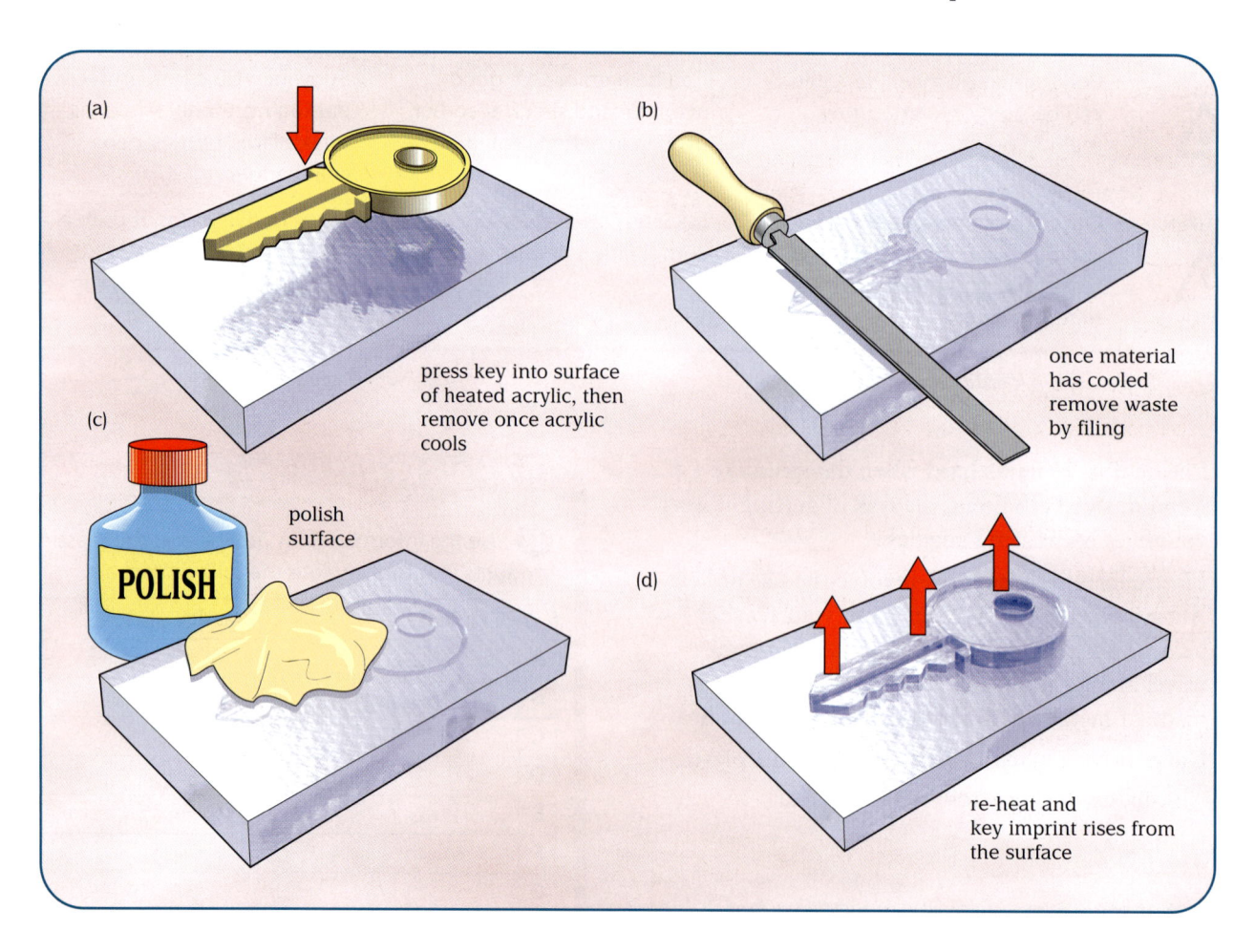

(a) press key into surface of heated acrylic, then remove once acrylic cools

(b) once material has cooled remove waste by filing

(c) polish surface

(d) re-heat and key imprint rises from the surface

42

Heating up the plastic once again will allow the shape of whatever was pressed into the plastic to magically appear once more. Thermoplastics can be compressed and then reform to their original shape when heated. This plastic memory makes it possible for this surface finishing to be easily achieved without complicated machining.

Plastic memory

Carry out the above experiment on a sample of acrylic and use large metal letters if possible to make your initials. Carefully polish the surfaces and then you can find a use for the samples! If not hang them all up as a class on cotton and allow light to pass through them in a window.

Plastics do not usually need a surface finish as they are resistant to corrosion from water and chemicals. However when handling them in the workshop, great care must be taken so that they do not get unnecessarily scratched.

Plastics are often available ready protected in a sheet of thin polystyrene attached to the surface to prevent such scratches occurring. This is then taken off when the final product is ready for use. Masking tape or paper can be used during manufacture too. For a final gloss finish however, a simple furniture polish or silicon spray can be used to catch the light and add that 'sheen' plastics so often have.

Plastics can look fantastic and lustrous when polished and care must be taken in order to achieve this result. A rushed surface on plastic can leave behind scratches and small abrasions that easily trap dirt and grease and leave the plastic looking rough and unattractive to the eye. Care must be taken to file away the scratches and them to smooth away the finer scratches with 'wet and dry' paper.

Patience is the key. You cannot hope to cover up the scratches with polish: it simply does not work because the polish will simply gather in the cracks and show up as dark greasy lines.

Plenary

Casting **resin** is a type of thermosetting plastic. With your teacher pour some resin into a mould and add the small amount of hardener needed to start the chemical reaction. It is important to get this percentage correct, as the resin will not harden if it is wrong). The mould can be a simple frame (approximately A5 size) made of wood that sits over a sheet of greased acrylic.

While the resin is mixing you can add coins, keys, beads, glitter and other small metallic decorations. The resin will 'set' and go hard overnight while keeping the small items mixed within it secure. The frame and the acrylic can be successfully peeled away to reveal the resin structure. Resins can also be coloured and shaped in a variety of different moulds. This plastic, like many others can be polished and made to sheen to catch the light and make an attractive piece of decoration.

Many designers such as Shiro Kuramata have used resin to make furniture in this way, go to www.heinemann.co.uk/hotlinks and click on this unit to see a picture of the Miss Blanche chair.

Product analysis

Objectives

In this lesson you will **evaluate** an existing product to inform your future design work.

Key words

evaluate	thinking about how and why products are made and how they function
objectively	looking at something without influence of personal feelings or opinions

At the heart of product design is the ability to look critically at a product and see how it looks and why it works the way it does. The skill of evaluation is something that is useful throughout your life. When you choose items to buy, ways to travel, a house in which to live, a bank account, and even what food to eat, you are evaluating these products. Think about the television programs you choose to watch. You like them for different reasons. You have evaluated them against your likes and dislikes. Designing works in a very similar way.

Product analysis is a very important part of design technology and can be carried out outside of the classroom. You may not realise it but every time you come into contact with a product you analyse it in some way. You make mental notes on its appearance, shape, purpose and size. If you look at it more closely you can begin to understand why a designer has developed the product in the way they have. It is good practise to collect different designs of a similar product and see how different designers have worked on them. You can learn a lot about design by comparing existing products.

By learning from an existing product, a good designer can avoid making mistakes and ensure the production of a successful new product. We all use coat hangers to hang our clothes on a rail or in a wardrobe. Have you ever looked **objectively** at the different types of hanger available (A)? Woods, metals and plastic, or combinations of all three, are common materials that are often used in the construction of hangers.

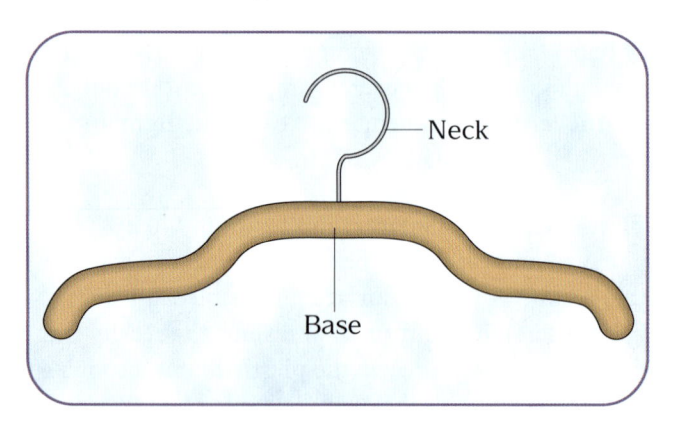

Exploring materials

Think about it!

PA Examine a sample hanger and then answer the following questions.

a) How many separate parts can you identify in a simple hanger?
b) Is there a neck, a base, a stem or any clips?
c) Are there attachments for other pieces of equipment?
d) How might the construction of the hanger increase the value of the item it holds?
e) How might the quality of the hanger reflect the quality of the product?
f) Is there room for a design label on the hanger?
g) How does the design of the hanger reflect the clothes it might be used for?

Redesigning something that already exists is a problem that all designers face at some point. Product analysis helps you to see what works in a design and what does not.

Think about it!

1. **PA** In groups, collect five different coat hangers. Consider the varying designs, shapes and materials. Draw and annotate a small part of each hanger, which serves the same purpose but looks different.
2. For each hanger, find one good point and one bad point. How could the hanger designs be improved?
3. **ABC** What materials have been used? Explain their physical properties. Why do you think these materials have been chosen?
4. **TS** Suggest why all coat hangers are approximately the same size.

You will come across the theory of product analysis time and again. It does not matter what the object you are exploring is, but the way you approach the object and the questions you ask about it. When concentrating on the coat hanger, you focused on its appearance, its manufacture and the way it performed.

These are the same type of questions you should be asking for any product when carrying out an analysis. Discuss the materials, the manufacturing process, the designed shape, the dimensions and how *well* the object operates.

Ask yourself are there any opportunities where you could have made improvements to the existing design and if there is a short falling in the object as it is at the moment.

Having answers like these about all products helps you assess your own work. If you make sure you carry out product analysis of your design when sketching and modeling, you will have a better chance of producing a successful idea.

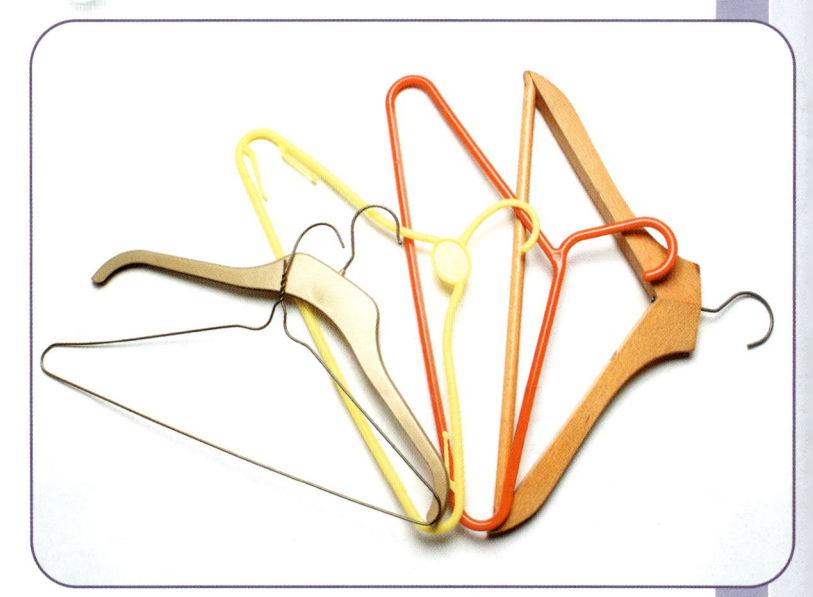

A

How many other types of hanger are available?

Plenary

Remember to have the answers to the following questions when carrying out a product analysis:

Who – who designed it?
Why – why was the object designed the way it was?
Where – where could the object be improved?
What – what is it made from, and why?
When – for what purpose was the object designed and how well does it perform?

Exploring materials

Hanging on

Objectives

In this lesson you will:
- design and make a product to hang or hold clothes or accessories
- identify appropriate materials for the task, considering appearance, function, safety and reliability.

Key words

specification a list of crieria that a new design must meet

DMA Hanging on

The design brief

To design and manufacture a product to hang or hold your clothes and/or accessories such as jewellery, ties or hair bands (A). The device can be free standing, hanging from the ceiling, hanging on the back of a bedroom door or fixed to a wall in the house.

Design specification

The product:
- should be made from a combination of woods, metals and plastics
- should be no more than A4 in size
- must incorporate two surface finishes, such as paint and varnish
- must contain a curve
- should be of your own original design.

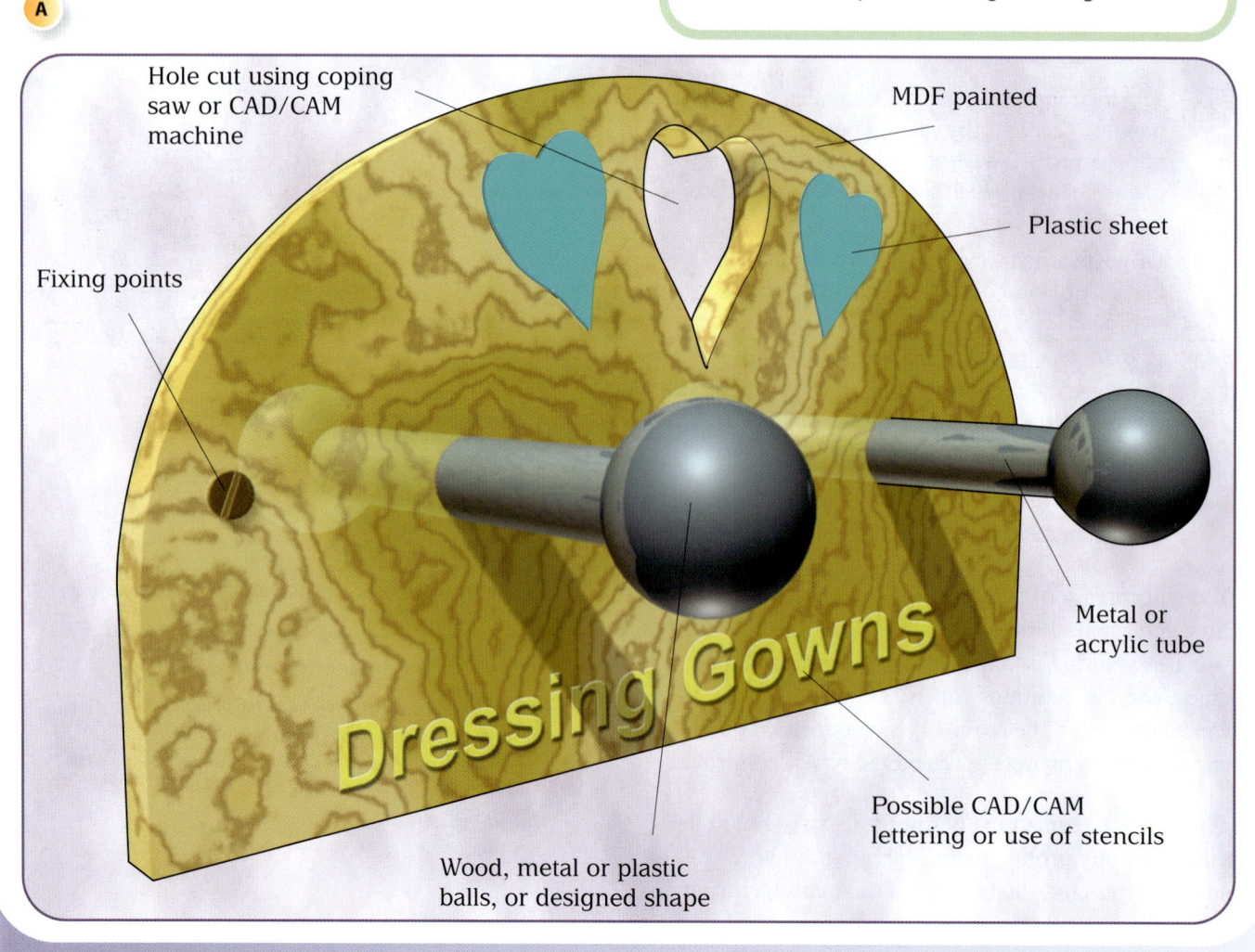

A

- Hole cut using coping saw or CAD/CAM machine
- MDF painted
- Plastic sheet
- Fixing points
- Metal or acrylic tube
- Possible CAD/CAM lettering or use of stencils
- Wood, metal or plastic balls, or designed shape

Exploring materials

🔵 Pattern focus

By combining two or three different materials in interesting ways and cutting them into different shapes, you will be able to create an imaginative and eye-catching product without the need to think of complicated ideas. If you are stuck for inspiration, think about combining simple squares and circles together, or add bends and curves to your design. This leads to patterns that are interesting and creative. Try not to copy logos or names, design your own. Use no more than two or three colours at a time. Overlap your sketches to create your designs.

How to come up with a fresh design

Follow the instructions given in 'Think about it!' if you are finding it difficult to come up with a profile for your design.

Think about it!

1. **CT** **D** Try this procedure to get some ideas for shapes, patterns or colours (B). If you have a suitable design package on your computer, use that to help you.

   a) Draw out some simple geometric shapes.
   b) Next, re-draw them overlapping in groups of three.
   c) Draw around the perimeter of the shapes.
   d) Join the shapes up with two or three lines.
   e) Finally, colour the shapes in using simple primary colours. Try using just one colour for each shape.

Plenary

Many of the world's best designs started as a doodle on the page. Practise doodling and sketching – you never know what you might come up with!

B

a) Start with simple geometric shapes

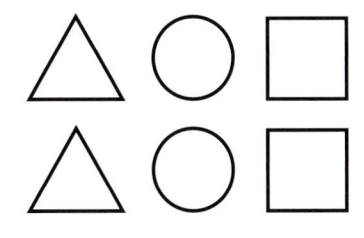

b) Draw them overlapped in sets of three

c) Draw around the perimeter of the shapes

d) Join the shapes up with two or three lines

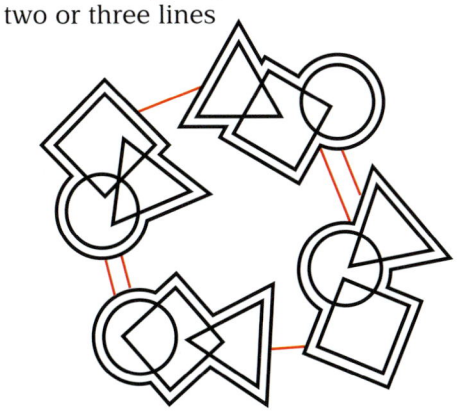

e) Colour in, in simple primary colours

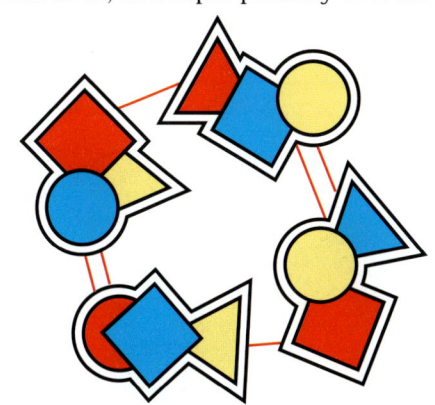

UNIT 6 — Designing for clients

Designing techniques

Objectives

In this lesson you will learn the main techniques that designers use to generate new ideas, including:

- mind mapping
- talking to people to gain information
- instant **modelling** with a variety of ideas
- taking everyday objects and searching for new uses for them
- using sketch books and folios to record thoughts and design explorations.

Key words

modelling	3D experiments that designers use to help them design
market research	the method of finding out what people like and need in a product

Mind mapping

Designers often draw a mind map to get all their ideas out as quickly as possible (A). This is a snapshot of all the considerations designers have in mind at the start of the project. A mind map can be in the form of words or drawings. Think freely and allow yourself to draw and write without restriction.

Product analysis

You carried out a product analysis task on the coat hanger in unit 5 (see pages 44-45). By looking at existing products, designers can gather important information that may help them with the design of their new product.

Market research

Sometimes the best questions to help you design are those that do not relate to the product you are designing. Instead you can find out what sorts of things people like and would purchase by conducting some **market research**. This involves asking people a range of questions, such as:

- what colours they like
- what music they like
- what shapes they like
- what books they read
- what makes them laugh
- what makes them feel different emotions.

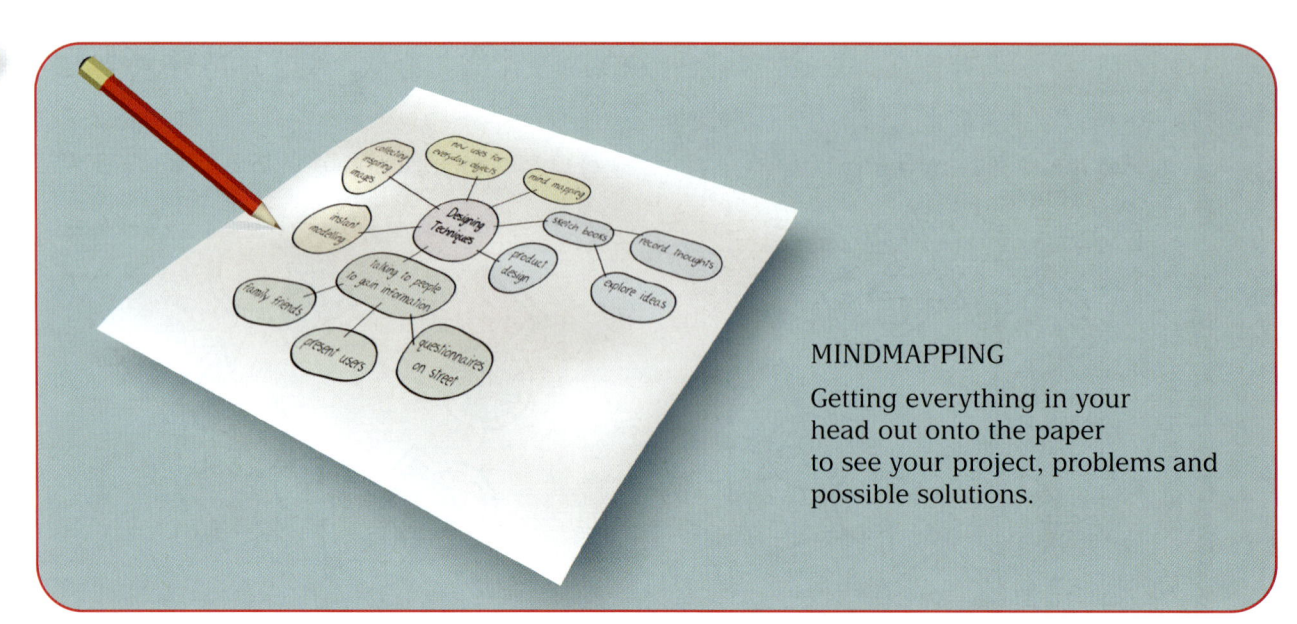

A

MINDMAPPING

Getting everything in your head out onto the paper to see your project, problems and possible solutions.

Designing for clients

B

Ask the people you interview (C) to create a mood board about themselves. Ask them to collect images, pictures, sketches, postcards and posters from books and magazines that they like. All these pieces of information help you get a feel for what sort style appeals to them. From this it is possible to create a successful design. Successful designers use this technique to create interior design themes for new homes.

C

Think about it!

1. Draw a mind map showing the many end uses for a bookmark.
2. **FPT ICT** Collect as many different bookmarks as possible. Try searching on the Internet for bookmarks using an image search engine such as Google. Go to www.heinemann.co.uk/hotlinks and click on this unit. Look for similarities and differences between them and make a note of the aspects which change from one design to another.
3. D Design a mood board showing all the things you like and which you feel will reflect you. Remember to include lots of images with colours and patterns, materials samples, photos and sketches.
4. Make a class display of your mood boards. Can you guess from other people's mood board what sort of person has made each one?
5. Collect five products that perform a function. Pretend that you have never seen these before and be imaginative when thinking of a new use for them. What could they be? Exercise your imagination!

Plenary

These techniques you have learned come together in designing and marketing to form 'blue sky thinking'. In other words, there should be no ceiling on what can be achieved.

49

Designing for clients

Design company: a case study

Objectives

In this lesson you will:
- investigate a real life design problem and solution
- make a comparison between your designs and the design process of a product design company.

Key words

PDD	Product design company: product innovation consultants
Exertris	product name: Interactive Exercise System
anthropometric	study of the measurements of the human body

The Exertris bike

Case study: PDD – Exertris: Interactive Exercise System

The projects and activities with which you have been involved have all helped you to develop your knowledge, and learn new skills and techniques. When you have been communicating to your classmates or teacher, through sketching or conversations your ideas have also been developing.

'Real life' design is no different. Designers and users are constantly communicating and discussing options and pulling together lots of different activities so that the best solution at that time, for any problem, can be found. **PDD** is a design constancy that specialises in production innovation. They come up with new ideas but follow the same sort of processes that you can easily recognise. PDD developed an exercise bike that differs from the norm because it involves the user.

The bike is different because it has interactive software and games, which are linked to the speed in which the pedals are moved. The games however are not associated with pedalling or racing. Gyms have found that users enjoy playing the games so much that they do not realise how hard they have exercised or for how long. See if you can follow the designing process with which you are now familiar.

Design brief

The client or user asked PDD to come up with a different way for people to exercise in the gym. The client had recognised that people who went to the gym were often bored or frustrated on exercise machines. Watching TV or reading distracted the user but did not involve them in any way and thus for some, exercising was sometimes monotonous. The initial idea for the design brief was to somehow use the popular 'exercise bike' style of machine to interact with gym use so users had a different experience when they went to the gym.

Think about it!

TS How have you worked from a design brief? What were your first ideas or thoughts? What would you do next?

Planning

PDD started with a plan that first identified all the important areas of the project. They needed to research into what people felt and needed when they went to the gym and what sort of machine would interest them or discourage them from use.

PDD also needed to work out how the mechanical aspects of the bike would function along with all the electronic interactions too. The bike would be used by all sorts of people so **anthropometric** data would have to be collected and used in the design of the bike. PDD split up their designers into teams to cover all these possible issues: a design team, a prototyping team and an engineering team. They worked to a nine month time plan and set themselves interim deadlines to stick to.

Think about it!

(TS) What projects have required you to split up the workforce?

Would brainstorming help you organize the project?

Why is splitting up the time important?

Researching and developing ideas

The design team used behavioural psychologists to observe people first hand at local gyms and ask them questions about how they exercised. It was discovered that large complicated looking machines put people off exercising. Research also discovered that people would react positively to a machine with a screen as they could interact with what they saw and felt 'connected' to the machine rather than just the recipient like they would feel if they were watching TV.

PDD took this information to develop their modelling and reviewed how their ideas had changed from initial sketches. This evaluation helped the designers to develop the final style, shape and appearance of the bike that would best suit potential users.

Think about it!

Why was it important to gather all this information?

Why was it important to review the initial sketches at the same time as adding ergonomic information to the developing ideas?

Where have you developed your ideas in projects in the past?

Planning production

PDD contracted Davall Gears to help develop a mechanism for the bike. A braking system was also an engineering problem that needed to be solved before production could commence. CAD modelling was used so that the operation and assembly of the bike could be tested before production began. Virtually creating the bike in 3D and 2D design packages enabled accurate data to be added to the design. The prototyping team could then use the information to finalise each component of the bike accurately.

Think about it!

(TS) How important were these factors in the design: safety, operation, comfort, appearance?

How might they have influenced the final bike shape and operation?

Why were computers used to test mechanisms and operations?

Why could a full-size working bike be made instead?

Why did PDD ask Davall Gears to develop a working mechanism?

Where have you used other people's help in projects before?

Where have you used standard components or CAD in your designs?

Production and evaluation

PDD extensively tested their prototypes by using engineers to explore mechanical issues and the designers exploring user reaction to the bike. These prototypes allowed a final blueprint of information to be used for the production tooling and assembly. The bikes can now be seen in many of the gyms up and down the country. Perhaps you know of one to take a closer look.

Think about it!

Why was the final bike not made first before people evaluated it?

Why was it important for the assembly and tooling required to be perfect as possible before production?

What materials would have been used and why?

What sort of texture would these material have and why?

What do you think of the solution PDD came up with? Is there anything that could be explored again?

Designing for clients

CAD/CAM

Objectives

In this lesson you will:
- learn how ICT influences designing and manufacturing in industry
- learn how computer-controlled systems are used in industry and commerce
- explore how repetitive quality can be ensured with CAD/CAM
- compare one-off and high-volume products.

Key words

CAD	Computer Aided Design
CAM	Computer Aided Manufacture

Computers have made a massive impact on the speed and accuracy in which products can be made. It is now possible to manufacture high-quality outcomes in a short period of time when previously people would have taken a number of days to make the same products with no guarantee that they would all be of the same standard.

Computer Aided Design (CAD)

CAD is a system that allows designers to create solutions to problems within a computer program through the use of illustrations. Designs can be modelled in 3D and manipulated time and again from all angles. There are many CAD packages available; your school may have a version.

Computer Aided Manufacture (CAM)

CAM is a term used to describe any activity where a machine is programmed with several instructions to produce a component from a raw material. CAD packages are commonly used through an interface software to drive the special machine codes that in turn tell the machine what to do and where to cut and shape the material.

A car has many thousands of components that all need to behave in specific ways. Cars have become increasingly complicated, yet each small piece of the engine or controls is relatively simple to make. This is because machines assemble and shape the raw materials or assist people in assembling them. Imagine how difficult it would be for one or two very skilled people to make these cars without the assistance of machines, computers, robots and diagnostic systems.

It is easy to imagine how a craftsman, equipped with hand tools, can manipulate hardwood into a well-made table or use metals to create some fine jewellery. In these cases, human touch and sensitivity toward the aesthetics of the pieces is easy to appreciate. However, computers are needed when manufacturing to consistently satisfy high demand and reproducible quality.

The major advantages to the designer and manufacturer when discussing the use of CAD (Computer Aided Design)	The major advantages to the designer and manufacturer when discussing the use of CAM (Computer Aided Manufacture)
• CAD is used to design complex products and components with ease. You may have accessed similar programmes for example AutoCAD, Pro/DESKTOP, Techsoft 2D, Inventor	• Can control many tasks simultaneously
	• Highly complex parts can be made in one machine sitting
• 3D design/virtual modelling is now the preferred method of design with 2D drawings being produced from the complicated image. This makes it easier to check that items will fit together prior to prototyping	• Greater accuracy is achieved – no human error
	• Greater degree of safety as no workers can interfere with moving parts during production
• A small number of skilled professionals can oversee the work of what used to take many skilled draughtsmen	• High produced speeds are achieved
	• Need for fewer operators – cheaper to run a business

Sophisticated computer systems can be integrated together to monitor every aspect of a manufacturing process. Designs can be modified time and again without the need to repeat all the drawings and computers can hold vast amounts of technical data with great accuracy. This information can be fed into a manufacturing cell where several robots or machines can carry out the precise tasks time and again precisely and with accuracy.

Computer Aided Industrial Design (CAID)

In CAID, computer designs are more commonly modelled in 3D and rendered to make the designs look as real as possible. The software is very sophisticated and more advanced than that found in schools.

Computer Aided Market Analysis (CAMA)

When companies wish to monitor consumer behaviour, they may use CAMA data to analyze their sales. For example, the use of bonus and reward cards in supermarkets provides information about what products people are buying and when they are buying them. This helps designers target new products.

Computer Numerical Control (CNC)

This is the control of machines using numbers or digital information. This can be provided manually or through a computer. Generally this is used for milling and drilling procedures. You may have machine at school with a CNC interface attached.

Flexible Manufacturing Systems (FMS)

A flexible manufacturing system involves the use of pre-programmed machines and computers to carry out a series of tasks and operations. They can be programmed so that a different set of operations can be carried out as the designs change.

Computer Aided Administration (CAA)

Here, data can be collected and accessed in a quick and effective way to assist manufacturing or information management. For example, your school may have an electronic registration system, or a company may use clocking-in identification to monitor the whereabouts of its employees.

Automatic Guided Vehicle (AGV)

This is an unmanned vehicle that follows a pre-programmed route around a factory floor or warehouse.

Think about it!

1. Copy and complete the first row of table C.

Object made by hand	Who is in charge of quality of finish and why?	Object made by computer	Who is responsible for quality of finish and why?	How this affects the consumer
knitted jumper		tracksuit top		

2. Working in pairs, think of three other examples of objects made by hand and by computer and complete the table.
3. **ABC** Write a report about the costs involved in making the products in your table. Think about costs of materials, labour, tools and equipment. Compare one-off production with high-volume production.

Plenary

When designing explore the possibility of having your product produced or drawn using CAD/CAM. You will find that your work takes on a more professional and high quality appearance.

Designing for clients

One-off production

Objectives

In this lesson you will:
- learn about one-off-production
- discover the importance of producing a prototype.

Key words

one-off production	a product required as a single item
prototype	a model or product which has been made to be tested or trialled before being put into full production

A

Ship building

What is one-off production?

You have been used to designing and manufacturing things for yourself. You were individually responsible for every stage in the design process, from the initial ideas to the final manufacturing. You needed to be skilled in every stage of the design process so that the final outcome was of the highest quality. You needed access at all times to a wide range of tools and manufacturing aids, and sometimes you may have only needed to use these items once. You worked from your own specification.

This type of manufacturing is known as **one-off production** or job manufacture. The tools and the processes used are sometimes referred to as plant. Examples of one-off production include shipbuilding, hand-knitted jumpers, homemade sandwiches, bespoke jewellery or an individually designed and made wedding dress (see photos in A). All these items may involve just one or two skilled craftsmen or a team of people all working toward one item. There is never a chance of a repeat order

Bespoke jewellery

Designing for clients

for these items. Sometimes large items may have massed-produced components within them, but the overall item is a one-off.

Characteristics of one-off production

- It is often expensive because the skills of the people involved are rare.
- It takes a long time for the items to be produced because of the design and all the stages involved.
- There is rarely a chance for the same product to be reproduced to the same specification.
- A large range of tools and plant is required, but may not always be used – such as when a carpenter makes fitted furniture for a house but does not use all his tools on every job.
- The items are often personal and may contain design characteristics that can be recognized.

Prototypes

A designer produces a **prototype** to bring to life (realise) his two-dimensional design work. It is a good way of seeing all aspects of the design to assess the proportion and function of the product before main production begins. A great deal of time and money can be saved at this time by producing a prototype. Famous designers Seymour and Powell make use of the prototype in the design process.

In many cases products are made with an end-user in mind. Prototypes can be used to gauge the end-users opinion, which will help the designer ensure they have met the specification of the end-user. Prototypes can be made quickly from any cheap material such as cardboard, foam board or coreflute and they can be joined together using hot-melt glue or stick-glue.

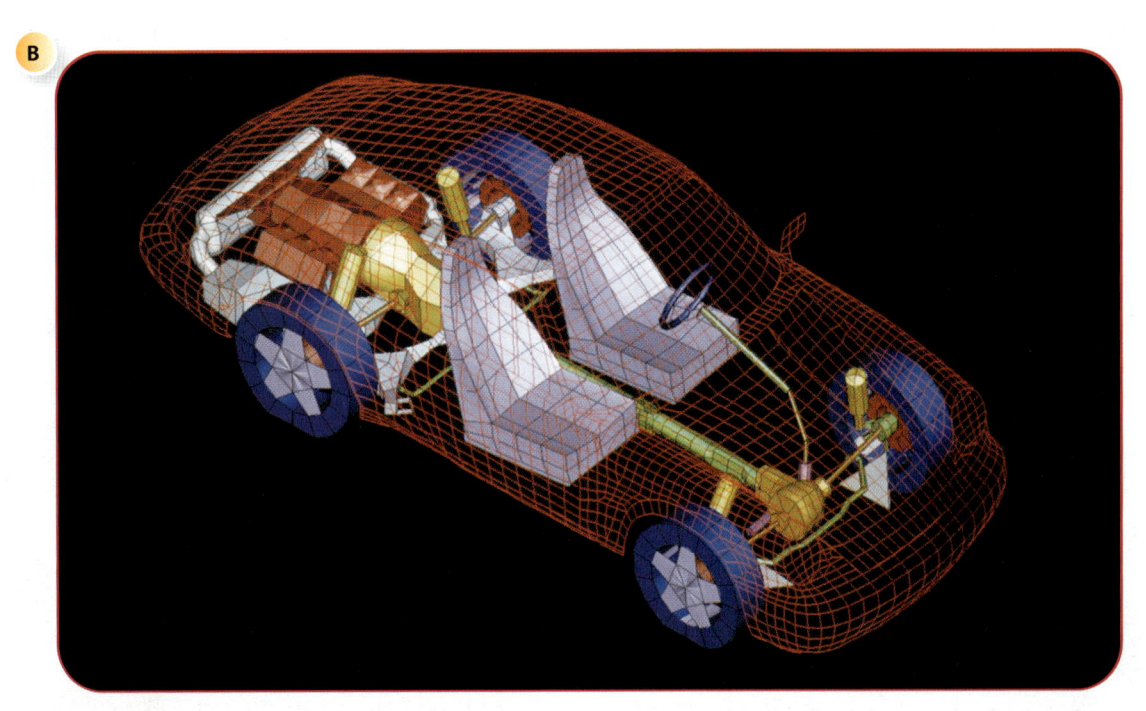

B

CAD/CAM allows designers to make prototypes so the design can be tested before it is built which saves time and money

Think about it!

1. **ABC** Have you made a prototype? If so, explain what you made and how it was useful.
2. Where have you seen prototypes?
3. Name three advantages in producing a prototype.
4. What materials could be used to make a prototype and why?

Plenary

Making card models helps a designer to realise the product being designed. It turns a two-dimensional drawing into a three-dimensional form. How many prototypes need to be made before the real product can be made?

Designing for clients

Designing using electronics

Objectives

In this lesson you will learn how suitable electronic components can be used to produce an appropriate and effective circuit.

Key words

Light Emitting Diodes (LEDs)	a small bulb used in an electric circuit
resistor	an electrical component used to limit the flow of current in a circuit
Ohms law	the method used to calculate resistance
solder	alloy consisting of tin, lead and flux
oxidization	when a metal reacts with the oxygen in the air
dry joint	a joint that is not permanently fixed together

A

How many different uses of light are shown in this picture?

In unit 4 you explored movement and its application in product displays to attract attention. Similar results can be achieved by utilizing the effect electrical current has on components. For example, lights in shop widows attract attention to the displays. Lights can also add atmosphere in a restaurant, theatre, cinema or home. Lights can be used within a safety or warning system, such as a fire exit, traffic lights, emergency services, emergency lighting and lighthouses. Spot lighting can be used to highlight specific areas of interest within a home or at a sporting activity (floodlights). A torch is a personal spot light.

Electronic components
Power sources – batteries and cells

A simple way to produce a safe power source is by using batteries which can be purchased in a variety of different sizes, with varying degrees of voltage, depending on what you want to operate. Batteries work from the reactions produced when different metals and chemicals are mixed. This is known as electrolysis. Batteries come in different sizes and ratings (B). You may be familiar with AA and AAA and PP3 sizes that power personal music centres and remote controls. These are rated at only a few volts.

B

Light emitting diodes (LEDs)

Light Emitting Diodes (LEDs) are devices that require only a small amount of voltage to work. They must be connected within a circuit in the correct way. They can come in a range of colours: red, blue, yellow, green, orange and white. LEDs come in different shapes and sizes, from flat and rectangular to dome shaped and cylindrical. Some LEDs can flash. They are relatively inexpensive but can be easily damaged if the current is applied across the two terminals incorrectly. LEDs should always be connected to a

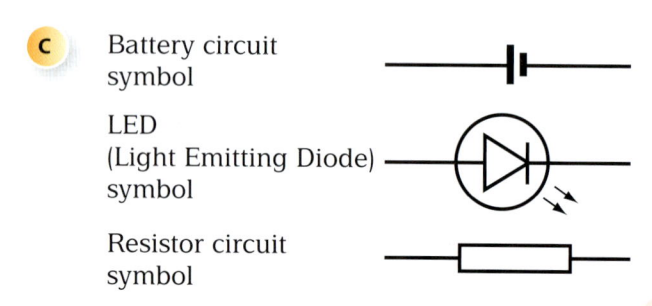

C Battery circuit symbol

LED (Light Emitting Diode) symbol

Resistor circuit symbol

D

E

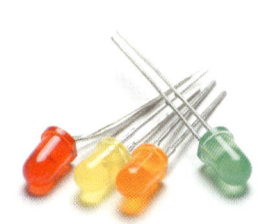

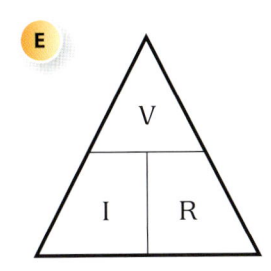

resistor in series if the voltage is larger than two volts. The value of the resister is calculated using **Ohms law** (I=V/R). Ohms law is commonly used to calculate resistance values in many circuits.

Resistors

These are small components used to limit the flow of current into a component within a circuit. They can be fixed values or variable values and come in a range of shapes and sizes. The resistors you will use for this project are easy to recognise as small peanut shapes with coloured bands around their circumferences. The resistor colour codes relate to the value of resistance each resistor has (F). Coloured bands are used because any wording would be too small to read.

Switches

Switches are used to make breaks in your circuits. There are many types of switches; you will probably be able to recognize rotary switches, touch switches, slide switches and punch switches in the classroom and around the home. In the next project you will use a Reed switch. A Reed switch is an electric component that consists of two metal strips that contain iron. The contacts within these switches are brought together using a magnetic field. You can find these switches in door and window alarms.

Solder

Solder is made from tin and lead which is held together with a 'flux' – a type of glue that burns away when heat is added. The flux also maintains a clean and electrically sound joint and reduces **oxidization** during the soldering process. This is important to prevent **dry joints** which prevent electricity flowing easily around the circuit. The heat from the soldering iron melts the tin and lead metal around the joints in a circuit to hold them securely when cooled.

Soldering irons

These are tools that are used to melt solder when constructing circuits. They heat the area in which the solder is to be applied as well as melting the solder itself. Goggles and aprons should be worn in a well-ventilated area to limit unnecessary injuries involved when soldering.

F

Resistor colour code

Resistors have four colour bands on them. The first colour band shows the first number. The second colour band is the second number. The third colour band is the number of 'O's after the first two numbers.

Colour		Number
Black		0
Brown		1
Red		2
Orange		3
Yellow		4
Green		5
Blue		6
Violet		7
Grey		8
White		9

Think about it!

In this project you will be using soldering irons. If handled incorrectly they could be a danger to you and/or others. Before you use them you need to think about all the possible dangers and what you could to prevent an unwanted accident. We call this a risk assessment and you will learn more about this in unit 8.

1. **TS** Look at the resistor colour code chart (F). Try to think of a rhyme to remember the order in which the coloured bands occur.
2. **123** Make a chart or calculator that will explain how to work out the resistor colour code.
3. **TS** Carry out a risk assessment of the soldering activity. Make a list of the hazards that are associated with soldering and how you take precautions to avoid being harmed or harming others.

Plenary

Try not to get confused or worried about the many different components you are using. A good tip is to begin by remembering what each individual piece is, before putting them into a circuit and then you will begin to understand why they are being used.

Designing for clients

Spot on!

Objectives

In this lesson you will:
- develop your manufacturing knowledge and understanding of plastics
- design and make a credit card-sized torch
- explore how the torch could be made as a batch or as a single item.

Key words

jig	a device manufactured to assist designers and makers to maintain accuracy when repeating the same operation time and again
template	a shape used by designers to draw around and mark up materials so that the same shape and quality of accuracy are repeated each time

You have already designed and manufactured products for yourself, but in this DMA the emphasis is on designing for other people. You will therefore need to be organized, motivated and support each other in order to complete the task.

A

DMA Spot on!

The design brief

- To design and manufacture a credit card-sized torch for personal use (A).
- The logo for the torch must be of your own design and should promote an imaginary company.
- The imaginary company has commissioned your class to manufacture twenty-five torches for release at a local business fair.

Design specification

The credit card-sized torch:
- should be made from a combination of plastics and electronic components
- must be no larger than 80mm x 50mm (so as to fit in a wallet or purse)
- must incorporate a high-quality finish with smooth surfaces and edges
- should be easy to operate and require no maintenance throughout its life
- should be easy to make within a batch production context
- be accompanied by a set of instructions for its safekeeping and eventual recycling / disposal.

FPT Production planning

Together with your teacher and classmates, collectively discuss the best production plan for the credit card-sized torch.

- You need to carefully consider the designing and manufacturing process so that the twenty-five torches all reach the same standard and are completed on time.
- You may also think about who has total responsibility for the project and who is in charge of sub-sections of the manufacturing process.
- Part of the plan could involve stopping production every now and again to hold quality control reviews.
- Remember that every member of the workforce needs to feel important and information needs to get through to everyone.

Designing for clients

Using jigs and templates

Using **jigs** and **templates** would increase accuracy, quality and the volume of products made. Jigs and templates can be made using materials such as wood, metal or plastic. When making jigs and templates, a great deal of care must be taken to ensure they are accurate. If a mistake is made on the jig and it is not put right, the production run will also have the discrepancy in it. A good way to ensure accuracy every time is to use a CAD package to design the template and then use a CAM machine to produce it or produce the whole production run.

A mould for a vacuum-forming machine is an example of a template. They can be produced by hand but in industry they are designed using CAD and made using CAM. An example would be the production of margarine tubs. Here many identical moulds would be produced using a CAM machine and laid out in a uniform manner on a large vacuum-forming machine so that lots of tubs can be produced at one time.

Polishing acrylic

A key element of the success of a project is its final appearance. The edges of acrylic are rough after cutting. They will need to be draw filed and then a selection of 'wet and dry' papers should be used to smooth the surface (B). Cream cleaner and metal polish and a lint-free rag can then be used to give the edge a high-gloss sheen. It may be possible for your teacher to demonstrate to you how a hot flame from a welding torch can also be used to polish up the edges of a sheet of acrylic.

A key feature of acrylic is its translucent and light-gathering properties. Acrylic is used as a reflective material in many light applications such as car headlamps. Your project could make use of these properties and hide a design within it or display a design in its outside.

Logos are on products so that customers can identify who it is made by. Often, products are sold purely because of their logo as they are considered to be fashionable. Some logos include the name of the company – others do not. Think about company logos that you are familiar with and identify the ones that display the company name within their logo.

Think about it!

D Design the logo for your Spot on! torch. Remember to be creative and not rely on simply copying logos or existing designs you see around you.

ICT Design your logo for your using a CAD package on the computer. Then, either

- print your design onto a self-adhesive sheet and attach it to your torch,
- or cut your design out of vinyl using Stika machine and attach it to your torch.

Plenary

Polishing the edge of acrylic takes time but leads to a professional finish. Tip! for extra gloss rub toothpaste over the edge of the acrylic and then polish it. Why does toothpaste give the plastic extra shine?

B

Polishing acrylic: firstly the edges are draw filed and then 'wet and dry' paper is used to smooth the surface

59

UNIT 7
Using control for security

Exploring control systems

Objectives

In this lesson you will design systems that control a range of output devices.

Key words

control system	a series of commands to obtain a desired outcome
pneumatic	control movements by the use of compressed air
hydraulic	controlling systems by the use of fluids
input	what is done at the beginning of a process
output	what happens at the end of a process

A

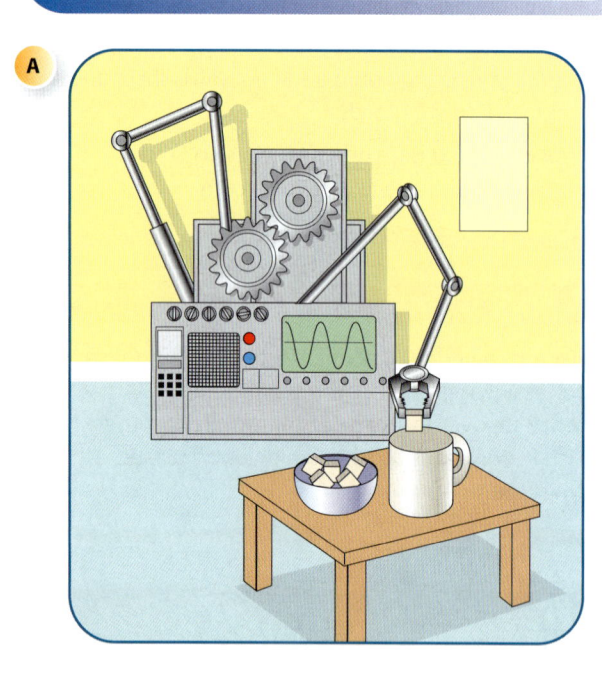

The main aim of this unit is for you to gain a greater awareness of **control systems**. These can be mechanical, electrical, **pneumatic** or **hydraulic**. You may have equipment in school that demonstrates how pneumatic systems can work. You may have already built small pneumatic circuits.

So far you have been encouraged to draw mind maps and express ideas and solve problems in a free manner. Good technologists not only have these skills, but they are also able to dissect large operational systems and use the individual parts as common building blocks for solving other dilemmas.

Some systems technology can also be demonstrated using computer interfaces and other electronic circuits technology. These are often in individual kits. Whatever equipment is available, the same building blocks of **input**, control and **output** are used.

Control systems

The use of control is common practice in Designing and Making Activities. You control a pencil by using your hand to draw a line. You control your stereo by using a remote control volume switch.

Through a completed series of commands, computers run programs with great accuracy and speed. But when these are broken down, they all use the same language of step-by-step cause and effect actions. Even the most complicated of control systems can be understood if you use the systems approach. This involves building block diagrams that state each stage of a control system. Look at this example of how to use a kettle to boil water (C).

If you repeat this technique many times over, even complicated systems such as those found in a computer can be understood. Any system can be broken down into easily understandable sections.

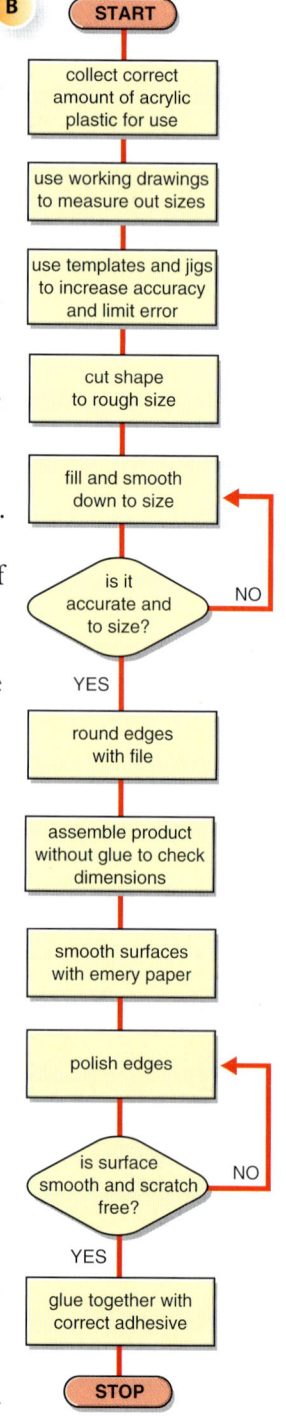

B

START → collect correct amount of acrylic plastic for use → use working drawings to measure out sizes → use templates and jigs to increase accuracy and limit error → cut shape to rough size → fill and smooth down to size → is it accurate and to size? NO (loop back) / YES → round edges with file → assemble product without glue to check dimensions → smooth surfaces with emery paper → polish edges → is surface smooth and scratch free? NO (loop back) / YES → glue together with correct adhesive → STOP

60

Using control for security

C

INPUT	PROCESS	OUTPUT
Fill kettle with water flick on switch	Element within kettle heats	Boiling water, switch off

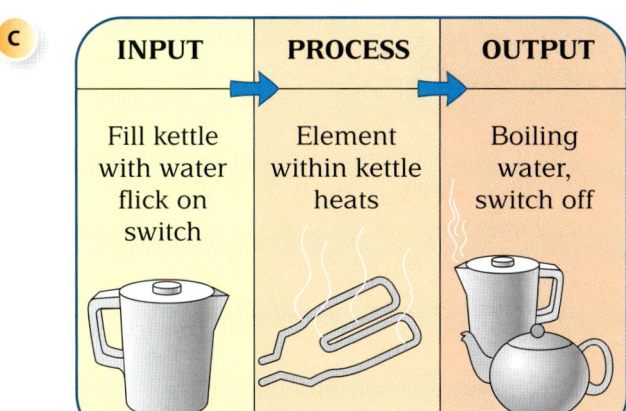

D

Toaster

E

Home thermostat

F

Stereo volume control

Changing a bike tyre

Feedback is needed to control certain systems. Feedback is a self-monitoring process that some systems employ to ensure the desired output is achieved and maintained. For example, a thermostat is used to control the temperature of a room (E). If it is too hot, you can turn the dial on the wall heater/mixer. You provide the negative feedback loop yourself. Another example of feedback is eating, if you are hungry you eat, there is a negative feedback loop which stops you eating when you feel full. Most examples of feedback are negative however, the howling in a PA system is due to positive feedback. The sound is picked up by the microphone and amplified and fed to the speakers which is then picked up by the microphone and so on. A volume control on a stereo uses feedback in the form of a listener. If the sound is too loud the listener will turn the volume down (F).

Think about it!

ABC Working in groups, create control systems for three of the following processes:
- making toast
- having a shower
- listening to music and adjusting the volume
- setting the temperature of your central heating at home or in the classroom
- finding a website page on the Internet
- changing the wheel on a bicycle.

Plenary

Control systems can be a complicated idea but, as you can see, designing systems to control output is not as difficult as it first seems. Can you think of any more examples of electronic and control systems?

Using control for security

Control systems

Objectives

In this lesson you will:
- learn about the use of input, process and output in everyday mechanisms
- investigate the application of simple security systems.

Key words

force — something that makes an object move

There are many different objects which you may take for granted that use mechanisms as a control system. Everyday objects such as door handles, tin openers, buttons on a keyboard, taps, scissors and pliers are all control mechanisms. Although they have been designed to do different jobs, they all have the same common characteristics.

- They make a job or task easier to perform.
- They all involve some kind of movement.
- They all involve a **force** of some kind.
- They need an input to work.
- They all have a form of output.

A

Photo A shows a picture of a speed clamp. It is designed to hold your work securely together but it also needs to be quick and easy for the user to operate. A speed clamp works in the following way.

- The muscles within your arms squeeze the handle mechanism and provide the input movement and force.
- The process is a series of linkages and ratchets that controls and magnifies the input force and closes the two jaws together slowly.
- The output is a constant and uniform force applied to your work at all times from the jaws at the end of the clamp.

The whole system can be reset by using a separate control system for releasing the clamp. See if you can explain the control system for releasing the clamp.

Simple security systems

You can design and manufacture simple circuits by adopting a systems approach. You can represent an alarm sensing circuit as a flow chart, as you saw on page 60.

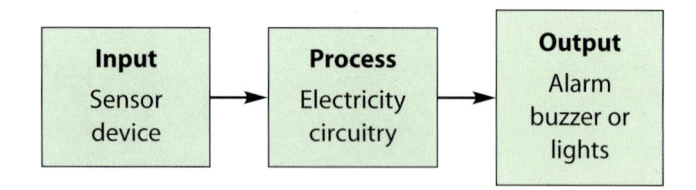

Input	Process	Output
Sensor device	Electricity circuitry	Alarm buzzer or lights

The sensor for an alarm could be:

- a light source that is broken
- a pressure switch that is trodden on
- a movement sensor or latch that is triggered when a window or door is opened.

Security systems rely on these simple building blocks as the foundations for the rest of the system.

The process in many security systems may be a complicated electronic circuit, but it will essentially always do the same thing which is to recognize that a change has occurred in the state of the sensor and that this change needs to activate the alarm. In some instances, a series of circuits that allows the user to identify where and what sensor has been triggered is needed. In this case, however, there will still only be one sensor to monitor.

Using control for security

The circuits in B work effectively and can be used to sense changes in light levels. In both instances the changes in voltages (input) in the circuit are detected by the transistor (process), which allows electricity to flow to the buzzer (output).

B *Dark and light detector*

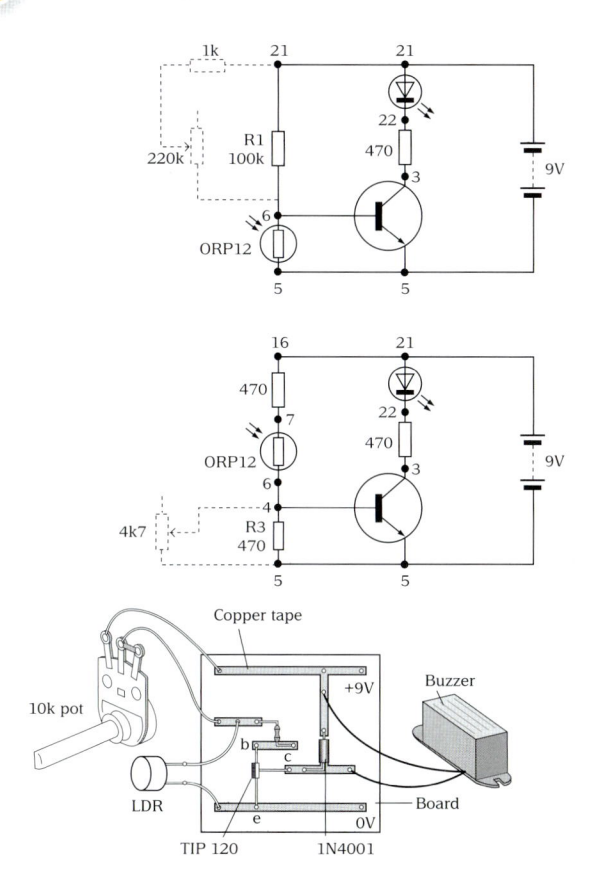

Think about it!

1. **TS** See if you can spot the different types of motion found in the speed clamp (A) or G-clamp (C).

2. **TS** Think about rotary, oscillating, linear and reciprocating motion. See if you can spot what motion operates the rear clamp and what motion exists as its output operation.

C

3. **ABC** Can you identify all the smaller building blocks in any one of the following alarm systems?
   - car alarm
   - house window alarm
   - fridge door alarm
   - wristwatch alarm.

FPT Alarm circuits

Draw the circuits (B) on card and replace the lines you have drawn with copper tape and solder the components directly onto the copper tape. It will then be possible to make the alarm go off when light falls upon it or when it is dark. This could be a simple way of protecting your folio from people opening it up and peeking at all your notes in the future! Both circuit variants are achieved by swapping over the LDR and resistor into alternative places.

Take care with the soldering iron! This simple exercise will stand you in good stead for the future where you will manufacture more complicated circuits from breadboards and printed circuitry.

Plenary

Now that you know about the different types of motion try to think of various ways that you can move your body to represent them. For example, walking forwards could be classed as linear motion.

Using control for security

Levers

Objectives

In this lesson you will:
- learn about the different types of lever and where they can be applied
- find out how mechanical advantage can be calculated
- learn what velocity ratio is
- learn what mechanical efficiency is.

Key words

lever	a mechanism that lifts, pulls apart or squashes forces
mechanical advantage	allows a user to move a large load without needing a large force
effort	amount of force required to lift something
velocity ratio	the relationship between input and output in a mechanical system

Levers are probably the oldest type of mechanism we have. We use levers all the time to open things which we cannot manage with our bare hands. Levers magnify force and concentrate it in one area. Levers can therefore lift, pull apart or squash together different forces.

There are three types of levers (see diagrams A, B and C):
- class one levers
- class two levers
- class three levers.

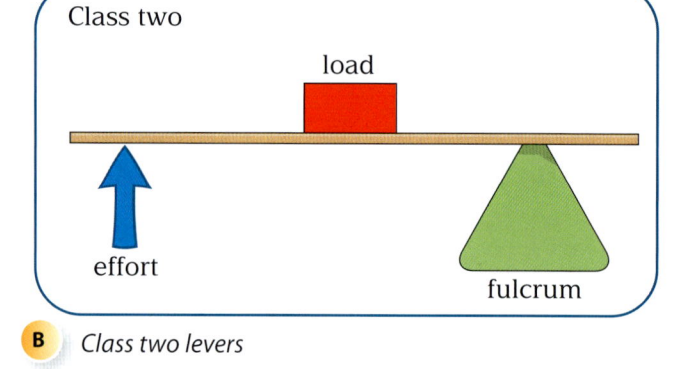

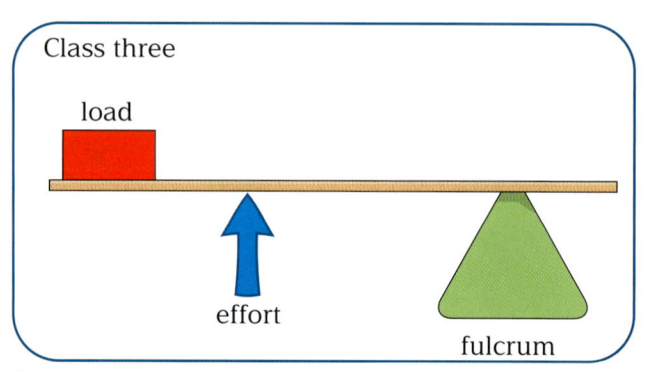

B Class two levers

C Class three levers

Mechanical advantage

A **mechanical advantage** allows a user to move a large load without applying a large force (see D). The mechanism essentially magnifies the input force so that the work is easier for the user to do. A mechanical advantage is calculated by comparing the weight of a load with the **effort** needed to move it.

It is usually the case that the input part of the system, operated by the user, will move more than the output part of the system will. The mechanical advantage is load divided by effort. In this case 50N divided by 10N equals 5N. This is expressed as a ratio, 5:1.

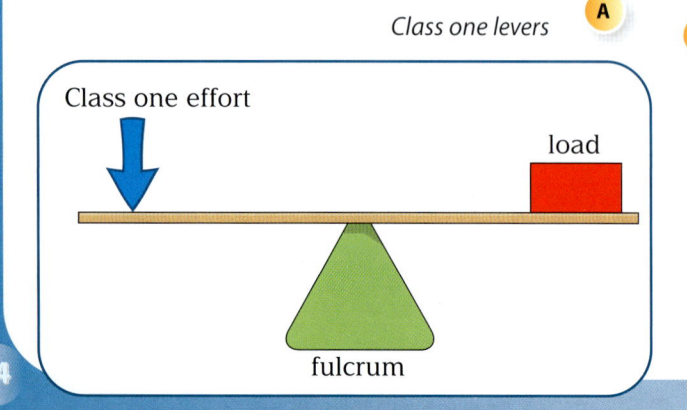

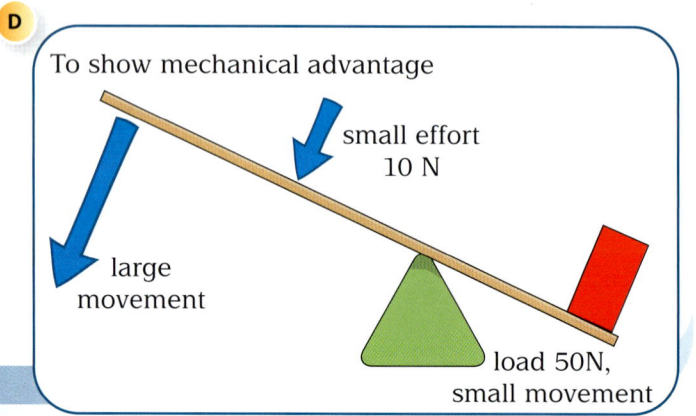

A Class one levers

D To show mechanical advantage

Using control for security

Velocity ratio

Velocity ratio is used to describe the relationship between the input force and the output force in any mechanical system. The distance an input force moves is compared with the distance the output load moves and is expressed as ratio. Look at a class one lever such as a wheelbarrow as an example. If the handles are lifted up 500mm and the distance moved by the load in the barrow is 100mm, then the velocity ratio is 5:1.

Efficiency

The efficiency of a mechanism can be calculated by the following formula:

$$\frac{\text{Mechanical advantage}}{\text{Velocity ratio}} \times 100\%$$

E

A vice and handle

Numeracy

When working with hydraulics you will use the following numeracy skills:

- You will calculate the volume of a cylinder from the area and length of tube
- Learn that load or effort = mechanical advantage
- Remember that $VR = \frac{\text{distance moved by effort}}{\text{distance moved by load}}$
- Remember that Pressure is $\frac{\text{force}}{\text{area}}$
- Consider effects, for example, the stilleto heel of a shoe worn by a petite woman still exerts the equivalent of one tonne of pressure
- When working with levers: remember perpendicular distance from fulcrum. In other words you need a small effort to move large load

Think about it!

1. **TS** Decide whether the following levers are class one, class two or class three levers.
   - wrecking bar, scissors
   - nut crackers, wheel barrow
   - hair grip, tie pin, tweezers

2. Why are mechanisms never 100 per cent efficient? What inherent problems are typical in any mechanism?

3. **123** Every workshop has a vice (E). Work out the mechanical advantage, velocity ratio and then the efficiency of a workshop vice using the numercay box formulas.

4. **123** What effect will lengthening the vice handle have on the mechanical advantage and the velocity ratio?

F

Which class of lever are scissors, hair grips and tweezers?

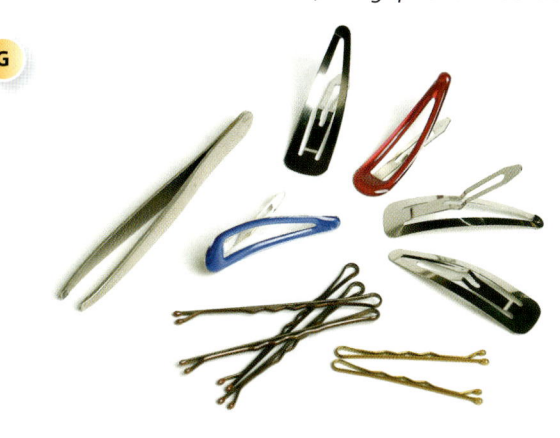

G

Plenary

ICT It is important to remember that levers are used everywhere to make your life easier, and have been used for a very long time. Search the Internet and see if you can find out who made the first lever calculations and how they used them to help design things.

65

Using control for security

Mechanical components

Objectives

In this lesson you will:
- understand how linkages change the direction of a force
- make things move at the same time and parallel to each other.

Key words

linkage	used to control movement and change the direction of force
bell crank	changes the direction of a force around a corner
fulcrum	pivot point
pivot	point around which an object turns
cam	object that sits on a crank and bring about a change in motion
crank follower	a supporting leg of a cam that follows a cam when it is rotated

A

Linkages

Linkages are used to control movement and change the direction of a force. They can also make things move all at the same time, or move parallel to each other. Often linkages do several of these things at any one time. Linkages such as **bell cranks** can be used to change the direction of a force around a corner.

Linkages can be used to change the distance moved, by moving the **fulcrum** or **pivot** along its length. You will find linkages in windscreen wipers, deckchairs, collapsible pushchairs, bike brakes, and ironing boards.

FPT Corkscrew model

Look at photo A, which shows a butterfly corkscrew bottle opener. Using thick card and paper fasteners make a large demonstration corkscrew to show how input, process and output works along with forces, linkages and fulcrums when the bottle opener is used.

- Label your model with the appropriate technical specification and describe how the mechanical advantage is achieved through the corkscrew mechanism.
- Make this A4 size so as it can fit into your folio as a revision guide later in your schoolwork.

Cranks, cams and followers

Cranks or **cam** mechanisms are used to change rotary motion to reciprocating motion. A cam is an irregular shape that sits on a crankshaft (B). When rotated, a **crank follower** resting on the top surface of the cam will move according to the profile of the cam. A follower is a supporting leg that follows the surface of the cam when the cam is rotated. Together cams and followers are used to change rotary motion into reciprocating motion.

Cranks and cams can be combined so that two motions are driven by the one common rotary motion. Followers can follow the inside track of a cam as well as the outside of its profile. Cranks supply a constant physical connection throughout. A cam follower can be shaped in different ways for different applications.

Using control for security

B

Bell crank

Pivot

Pivot

Linkage

Effort

Pivot

Cams

Pear shaped cam

Circular cam

Crank follower

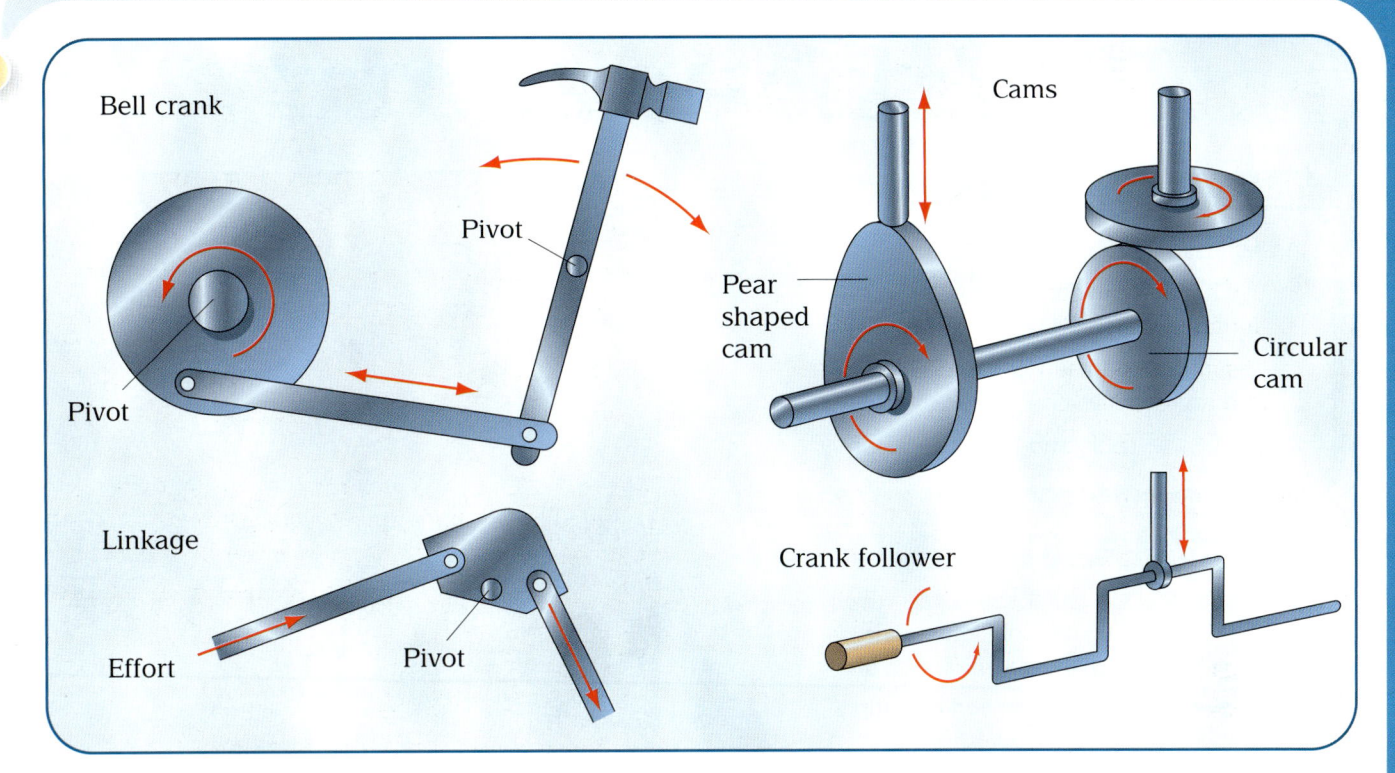

Think about it!

All of the mechanical components we have looked at can be found in any car today. They have all been cleverly combined to provide us with a product that has revolutionised the way that we travel. Can you imagine what modern life would be like without the motor vehicle?

Plenary

Have a look through a car manual at the detailed schematic drawings of the engine. Make a note of how many mechanisms you can see. Can you spot a cam, crank, lever and linkage?

CAM profile

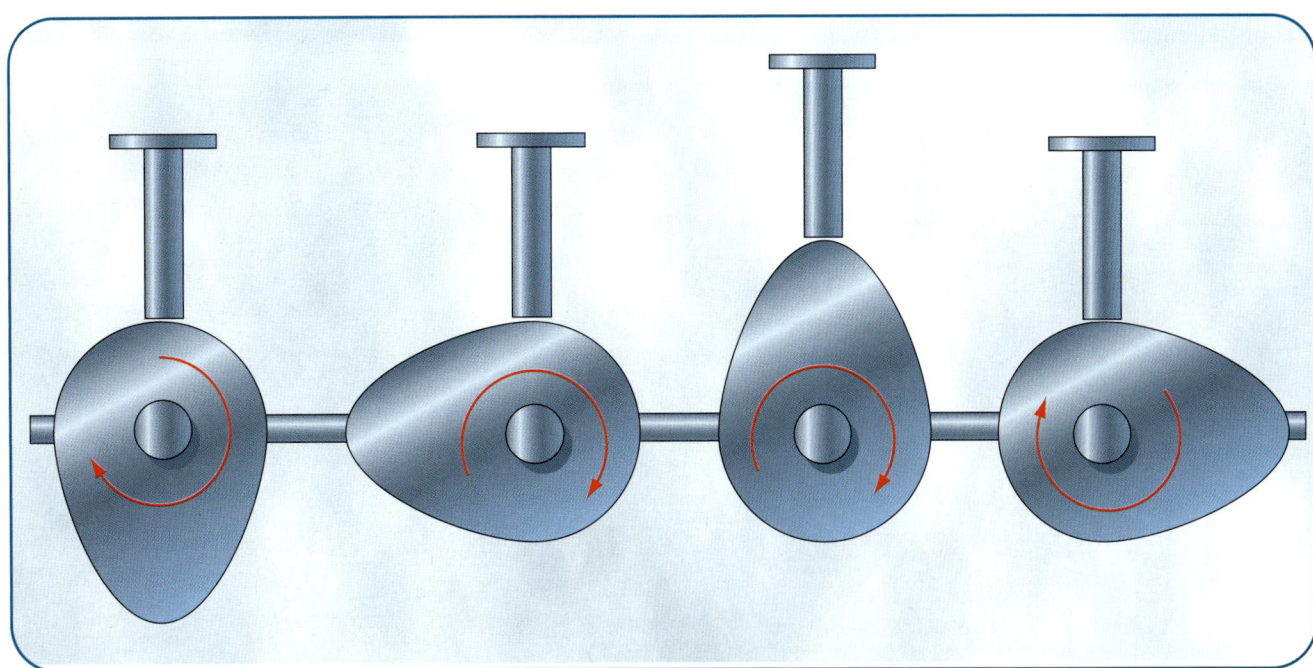

C

Using control for security

A bug's life – design brief

Objectives

In this lesson you will:
- use a simple micro-controller to control lights, sounds and movement
- design a bug based on the TEP bug kit and an IQ micro controller
- work with tools and equipment safely.

Key words

micro-controllers	small computers which controls light, sound, movement and so on
animatronic	making and operating life like robots
TEP bug kit	a kit to help you create a bug available from TEP

You may have a collection of moving toys that make use of electronics to enhance their appearance and performance. Toys have evolved rapidly from the day of simple building blocks or wind up vehicles. Many of today's exciting toys use cheap **micro-controllers** to make them walk and talk and behave as if they were real. It is possible to use this technology in schools to design and manufacture robot-like mechanical toys for project work.

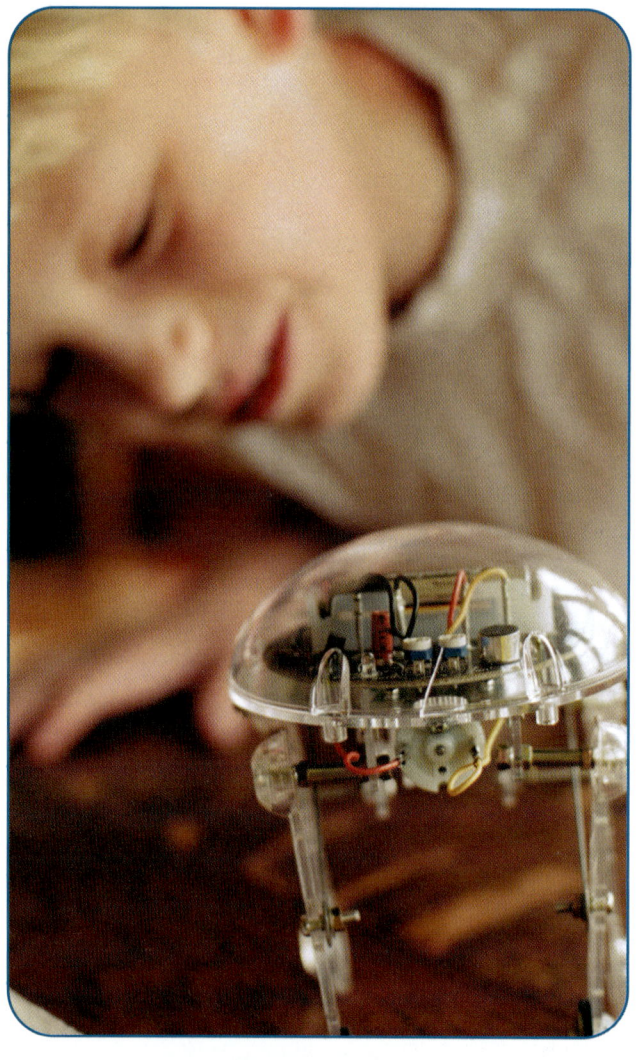

Using control for security

DMA A bug's life

Design brief

You are going to investigate a variety of ways in which a simple micro-controller can be used to develop an **animatronic** creature. This micro-controller can be pre-programmed so that it commands a series of outputs to make the creature move in different ways.

The creature feature you made in unit 3 was static and decorative. The only differences in its appearance were different items being held in its clothes peg mouth. The creature in this project makes use of electronic control and a series of different behaviours can be programmed into the controller.

The project is based around the **TEP bug kit** and makes use of the IQ micro-controller. These kits can be used to make different projects in the same way that some mass produced products made industrially make use of similar standard component to perform different operations.

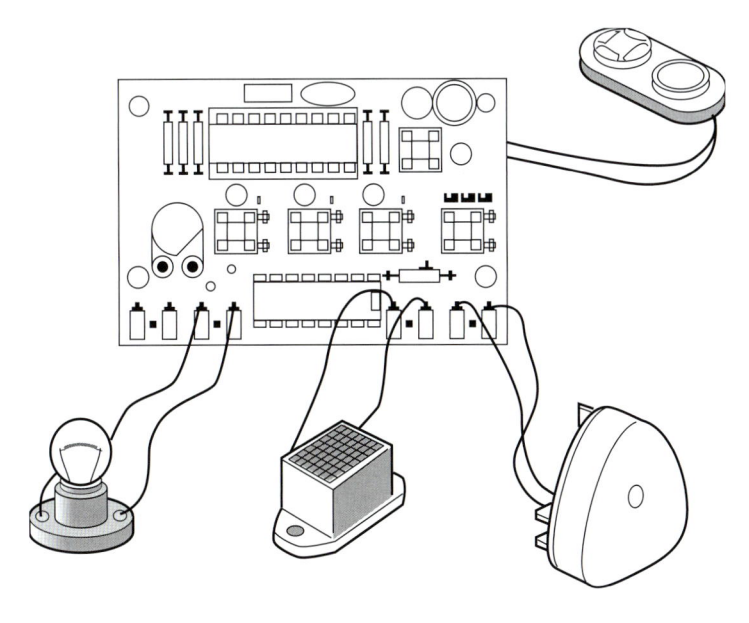

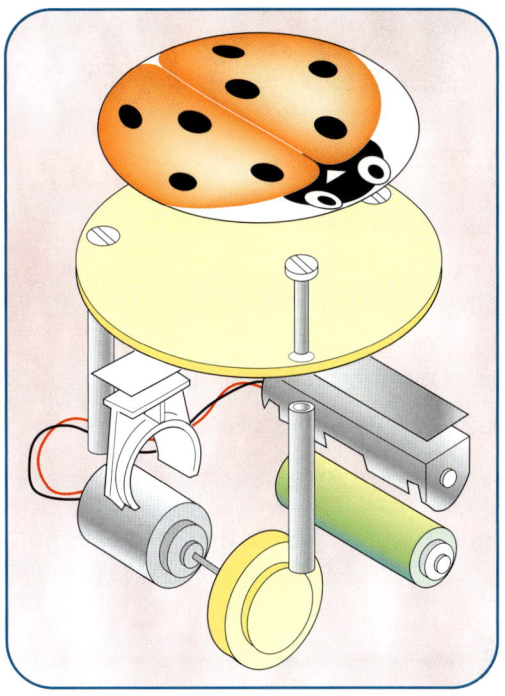

The TEP bug kit

You will need:

- TEP bug kit
- IQ board
- Input switches – toggle, micro-switches, magnetic switches and so on
- Output devices – bulbs, leds, motors, buzzers and so on
- Drivers – various transistors and resistors
- Coloured card / acetates
- Corrugated card
- Wire, solder, soldering irons and so on
- Batteries
- Vacuum forming plastic

The IQ micro-controller

Plenary

Identify in the home where micro controllers are found in the following situations:

- cooking food
- heating the home
- securing the home
- providing entertainment
- managing resources / time.

Using control for security

A bug's life – programming

Objectives

In this lesson you will:
- plan the design and manufacture of your bug
- use a suitable sensor to respond to external events and trigger sequences.

Key words

a bi-colour LED — a red and green LED with two leads, only one LED can be on at any time

Now that you have the design brief and equipment ready to make your bug we need to begin to programme the IQ micro controller.

The overall project can be broken down into small achievable tasks that can be achieved by a team rather than an individual. Planning the project will require you to use the resources in an effective sequence, plan the design and the manufacture so that everything can be achieved and understand how the electronic controller works so as all members of the team can make use of its functions in the designing stage.

To help you throughout the project there is plenty of advice that can be found on the DATA'S ECT and TEP websites which can be reached by going to www.heinemann.co.uk/hotlinks and clicking on this unit. Use these websites to access new information.

Here are some ideas for your animatronic:

- Cover the bug with a fabric shape
- Use cut-down pop bottles as the body of the bug
- Add antennae (for example made from plastic tubing with lights at the end)
- Make eyes light up by using lamps or LEDs
- Make a noise by using a buzzer

The IQ micro-controller

The IQ micro-controller is a small inexpensive programmable controller. It is a way of embedding intelligence into some of the electronics and control products that you will be using.

Look at the IQ board and you will see the following:

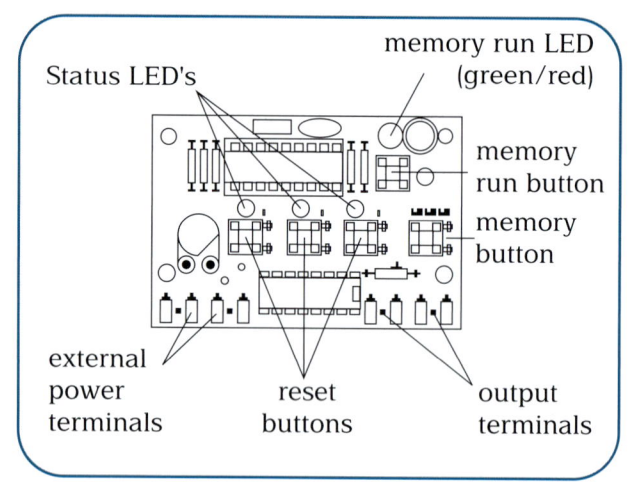

IQ board — Status LED's, memory run LED (green/red), memory run button, memory button, external power terminals, reset buttons, output terminals

Programming the IQ

The IQ controller can be used to control motors and lights in order to make your bug appear real. Learning how to program the IQ micro-controller does not take long and once mastered it should be easy to identify how to add a sequence of events to your controller.

These events will be seen as 'behaviours' for your bug.

Use the controller to control motors and lights and buzzers and so on to give your bug 'life'.

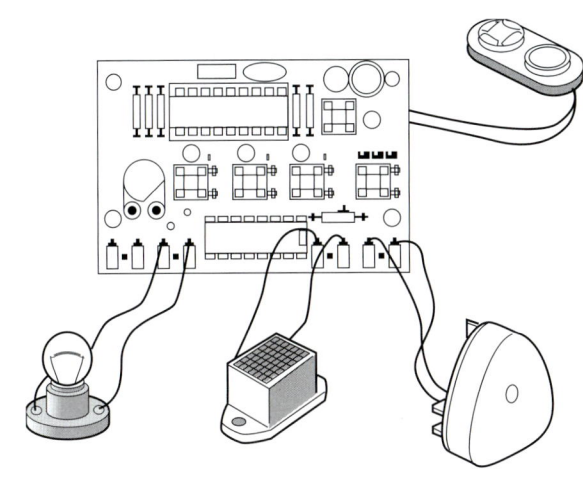

Using control for security

The IQ micro-controller

When the battery is connected to the IQ board the memory/run LED will flash green and then turn red. It is now possible to start programming the card.

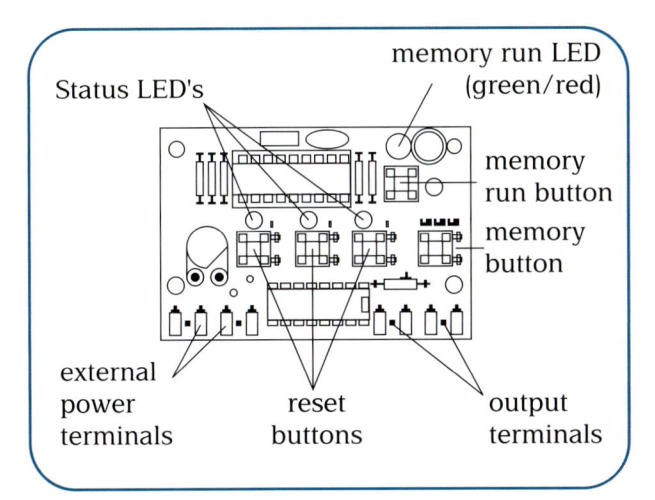

IQ board

Programming the card

- Press the left hand set/reset button once. The first LED comes on. Pressing the set/reset button again turns the LED off.

- This set/reset switch is an example of a 'toggle' switch – it allows you to toggle or alternate between two different signals.

- Then press the memory button on the right hand side. This stores your decision in the on-board memory chip.

- Press the middle set/reset button – the middle LED should come on.

- Then press the memory button on the right hand side.

- Keep pressing the set/reset buttons and press the set memory button each time to enter your choice in the memory chip.

- When you are happy with your decisions, press the memory/run button. The memory/run LED will change from red to green. (This LED is an example of a **bi-colour LED**).

- Watch the LED's display the pattern you have entered.

It is this pattern of adding information bit-by-bit and in sequence that allows you to build in all the behaviours for your moving creature.

It is important to see that the project hinges upon your designing skills and creative skills with the controller as the centre of your project. Any motions and movements or 'behaviours' that you programme into the bug are as important as the decorative nature of the bug.

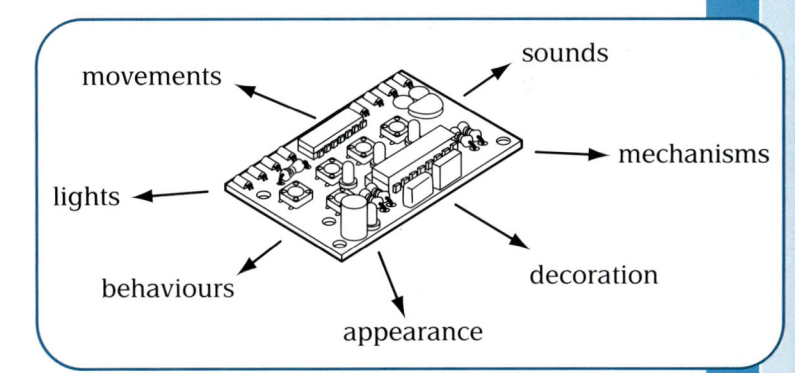

The IQ controller can create many behaviours for your bug

Plenary

Can you think of other products that use micro-controllers? How would you change their 'behaviour'?

Using control for security

A bug's life – assembly

Objectives
In this lesson you will demonstrate a number of simple construction techniques to complete the design of your bug

Key words
evaluate   thinking about why and how products are designed and made and how they function

Assembling the bug project

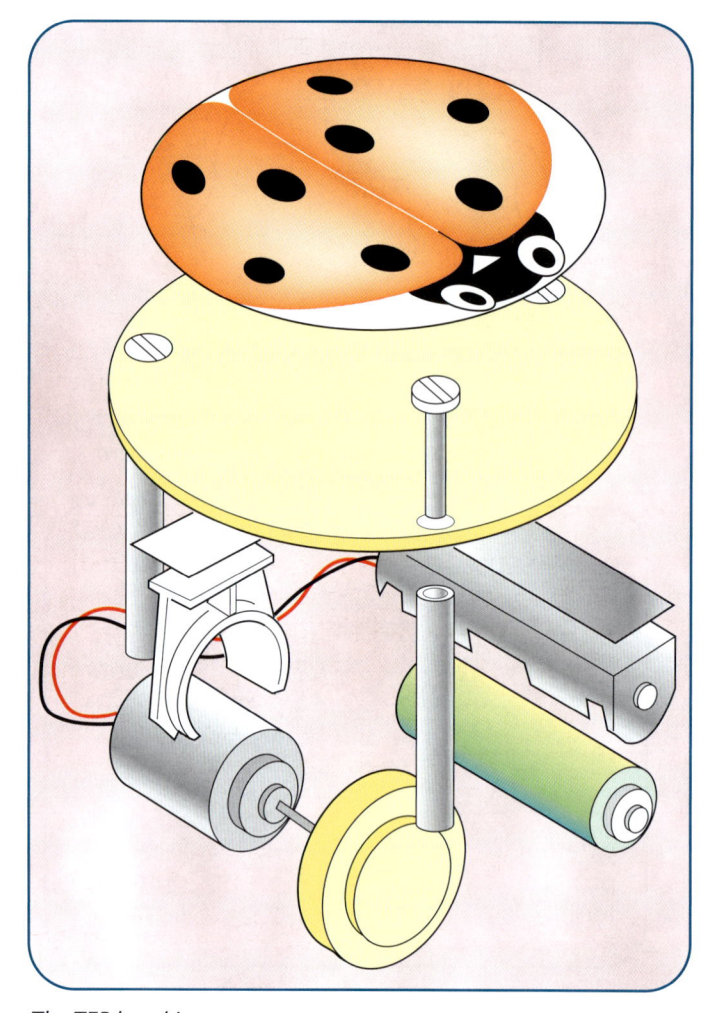

The TEP bug kit

Now that you have programmed your bug you need to design the shell to accommodate it. For example it is important that if the arms of the bug are going to move that you design arms that can move successfully in order to show off that feature. The TEP bug kit is a starting point, but try and use these kits as a half way point rather than assemble what has already been done for you.

Think about it!

TS New or old technology?

There are few examples of 'new' technology in the world. Systems have simply got better. An engineer from 1850 would be able to appreciate the workings of a modern engine, as the science has not changed, it is our manufacturing abilities that have improved. We can actually manufacture what we could only once conceive.

Could an Egyptian or a Greek appreciate the workings of a clock? Has the clock really changed in it operation in the last hundred or so years?

Now you have successfully experimented with the controller, you need to explore the actual body of the bug. For example will the bug need space to carry the controller and battery or could it somehow be carried in another way?

> **Think about it!**
> How many products can you think of that use electronics such as micro-controllers? Where is the micro-controller carried? Is it always part of the design?
> Remember you need to account for space for the micro-controller in the design of your bug.

You need to agree with members of your team the size of the bug and the amount of moving parts needed. For example you may decide that the bug should not be larger than a maximum size and contain no more moving parts than two or three. The number of lights, buzzers and movements will restrict the designing, you need to make sure that your design is broken down into manageable activities rather than being so large that the task is incomplete at the time of assessment.

You have explored in previous units how emotional and imaginative design can result in successful and interesting products. Setting constraints and restrictions for a project is also a technique that allows successful designs to be achieved and may help your team focus on the task at hand.

Once you have designed the shell of your bug it is time for assembly. Try to make your bug as individual as you can and take care with the final assembly, work as a team and plan all of your assembly carefully.

Evaluation

Now that you have designed, programmed and assembled your bug it is time to evaluate your work. Use these questions to help with your evaluation.

1. How successful has your team been during the design and making of the bug?
2. Did you save time working as a team?
3. How could this process be used in industry?
4. What would you do differently if you were to use the IQ micro-controller again?
5. Would you make any changes to the overall design of your bug?
6. Would you change the assembly or programming process at all?
7. Why did you make the decisions you did about behaviors and construction of your bug?
8. Did you modify any of your ideas during the project?

> **Plenary**
> Could the IQ controller be useful in your point-of sale display from unit 4? Can you think of other projects where control systems could help your design?

UNIT 8 Producing batches

Manufacturing with MDF

Objectives

In this lesson you will:
- learn how to make and produce items in quantity and to a high standard
- find out how manufacturing items in batches and using jigs allows you ensure a high quality outcome as the end product
- consider how extraction and the use of MDF affects the natural environment and human health.

Key words

varnished	a glossy finish to a surface
veneered	thin layer of wood, plastic and so on used to cover a surface to improve appearance
lacquered	a protective coating applied with a brush or aerosal
laminated	coating of thin layers

In this unit you will produce an item of storage in quantity as a class project. The two key elements of the project are the time spent in setting up the production system (the production run) and the achievement of accuracy in production. The main material used is likely to be MDF. The physical properties of this material makes it an ideal choice for this application, so it is worth reviewing our knowledge and understanding in greater detail.

MDF

Medium Density Fibreboard (MDF) is made from pulped wood, scrap wood and loose cuttings from the wood industry; even paper and card can be used. This is combined with a formaldehyde-based resin. This mixture is then rolled and pressed together to form large sheets of stiff, hard and uniform thickness board. The advantages of MDF over natural timbers are that:

- there is no grain that may weaken the board
- it comes in large sheets that negate the need to combine several sheets of timber together
- it can be sanded in a short time to achieve a very smooth surface finish
- it is uniformly the same thickness throughout
- it is as strong in all directions
- it can be painted, **varnished**, **veneered**, **lacquered** or **laminated** in several finishes to suit the requirements of the user
- it is relatively cheaper than natural timbers in large quantities
- it can come in fire-retardant or water-resistant forms
- it can be easily cut by machine tools without splitting
- it will not warp, bend, twist or create shakes and has a very low moisture content.

These properties of MDF have made it a very popular material used by many interior designers on contemporary television design shows.

A

'Handy Andy' is a popular TV presenter famous for using MDF

Possible health issues of using MDF

As the glues used to bond the wood pulp together are resin-based, there is a concern that people's lungs cannot break down the dust effectively when MDF is cut (B). Unlike natural timbers, where the wood is largely carbon-based, MDF dust is very fine and has higher concentrations of chemicals not related to the wood sources. This has led to some concern that operating and manufacturing with MDF poses a significant health risk to those involved.

It is therefore important to reduce the amount of dust you are exposed to at any one time. Extraction systems within your school should be extracting the wood dust away at source and maintain a clear supply of air through the workshop (C). Goggles and masks should be worn at all times.

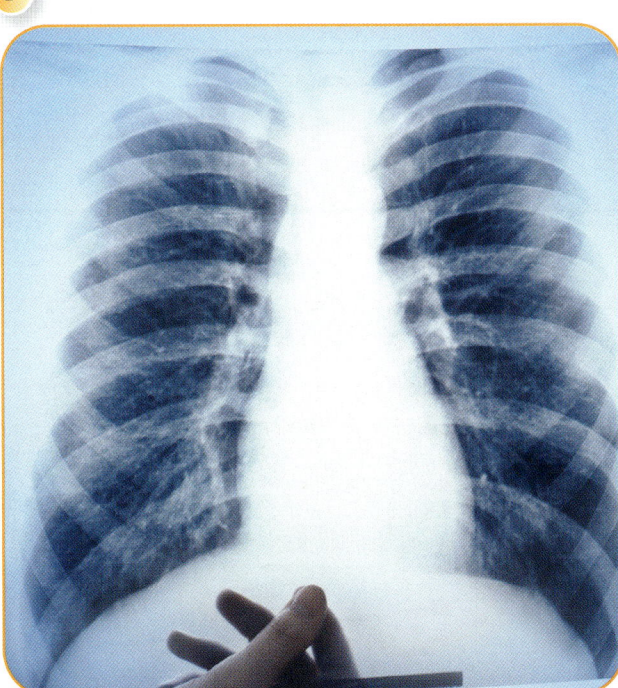

B

X ray of a person's lungs

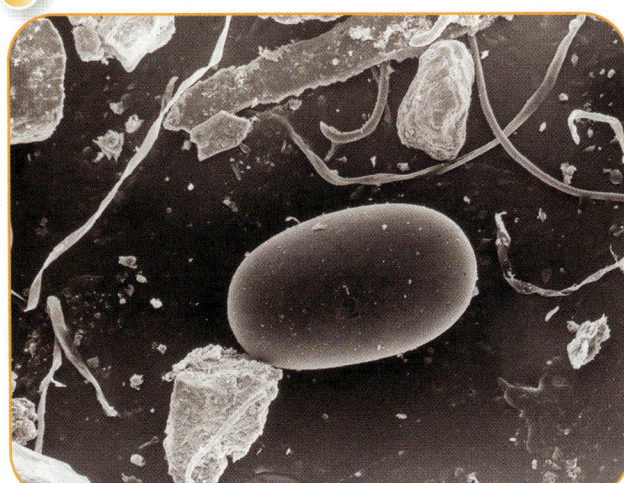

C

Dust particles

MDF Tests

Ask your teacher for ten pieces of MDF about 30mm x 30mm. Carry out a series of tests on them and display your findings as a wall mounted information board. You could work in pairs for this exercise. Here are some suggestions for tests:

a) How long does it take for water to seep into MDF?

b) Does vanish dry quicker when applied to the end grain or the front surface?

c) What paints work best on MDF?

d) Are there different grades of MDF? If so what are they?

e) How many different thicknesses of MDF are there?

f) What surface provides the best bonding area, is it end grain or front surface?

Think about it!

Consider the risks involved in working with MDF. For each of the jobs listed below, write down the possible risks and what you would do to minimize them:

- drilling
- cutting
- sanding
- painting
- marking out
- moving materials from one place in the workshop to another
- storage and retrieval.

Plenary

Where could you use fire proof MDF? Is it expensive? If it is why do you think this is so?

Producing batches

Risk assessment

Objectives

In this lesson you will:
- consolidate your understanding of safe working practices
- learn how to make a risk assessment.

Key words

hazard	an event that could cause harm to someone
risk	the liklihood that a hazard will occur

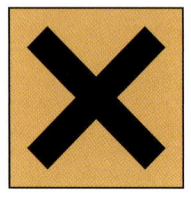

A manufacturing plant is a potentially dangerous environment. The more people working there, the more likelihood there is of an accident. A **hazard** is an event that could cause harm to someone. A **risk** is the likelihood that that hazard will occur. A useful exercise is to do a risk assessment for your project manufacturing. If you can identify where the accidents could occur, then you can take steps to avoid them happening. For example, cleaning away your tools, sweeping down the bench and wearing aprons are all things you should now be familiar with.

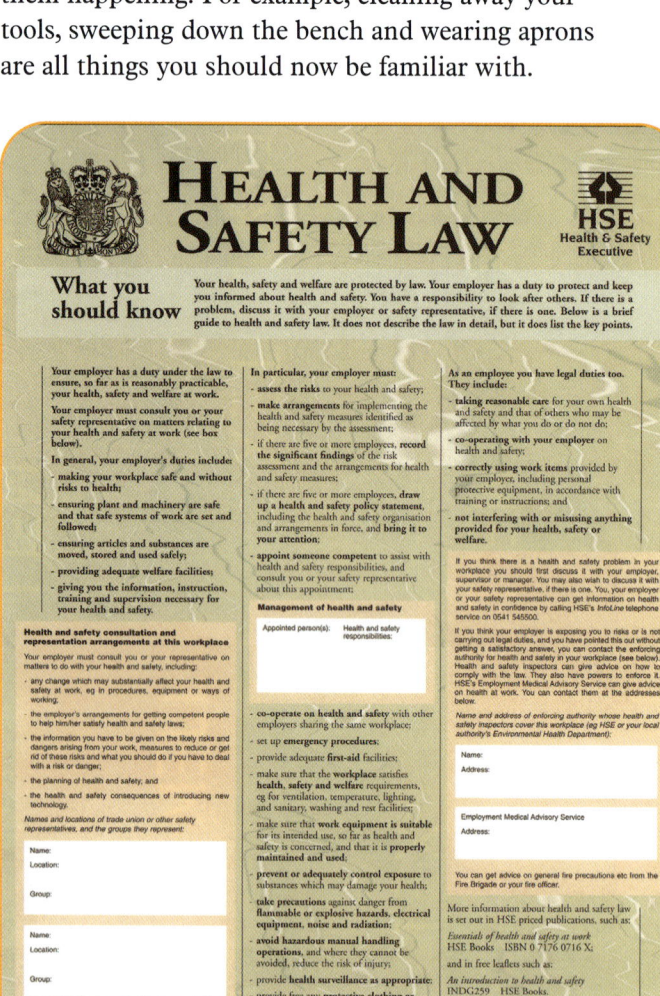

A

Producing batches

B

C

Plenary

Risk assessments are carried out to ensure your safety. You carry out a risk assessment every time you cross a busy road, if you did not you would be putting yourself in great danger. You have to apply the same risk assessment criteria when designing and manufacturing your products.

Think about it!

1. **ICT** Look up the Health and Safety at Work Act, 1974, and find out who is responsible for carrying out risk assessments and why they are carried out.

2. Carry out a risk assessment in your own classroom before you start work. Complete the table below to help you carry out a risk assessment, an example is completed for you.

3. Illustration B shows a picture of a classroom with a great deal of activity occurring all at once.
   a) Working in pairs, see if you can identify the possible hazards and risks that are occurring at any one time.
   b) List who is at risk and describe what steps are needed to reduce the chances of them being harmed.

4. Imagine you have been asked to give instructions to a new member of the class on how to carry out a risk assessment of one of the following procedures:
   - drilling MDF
   - bending acrylic with a strip heater
   - using a chisel
   - using a scalpel and safety rule to cut card.

   Write a step by step guide and remember to include all the safety considerations you can think of.

5. Look at photo C. Working in small groups, identify the potential hazards and risks in this manufacturing unit.

Activity	What is involved?	What are the hazards?	Who is at risk from these hazards?	What steps are taken to minimize the hazard from occurring
Using a pillar drill	Drilling through timber/plastic or metal using a high speed drill	• Entrapment • Flying debris • Hot shards and splinters • Spinning machinery with high torque	Pupils operating without training or supervision	• Clear instruction • Use of goggles, apron, clamps, knowledge of emergency stop location • Clear working space • Staff supervision • What to do in an emergency • No distraction from class mates

77

Producing batches

Batch production

Objectives

In this lesson you will:
- learn about batch production
- carry out a practical investigation and batch produce a small quantity of identical products
- learn how manufacturing aids are used in volume production.

Key words

batch production	a method of production where a number of parts are all made at once by several different people
template	a shape used by designers to draw around and to mark up materials so that the same shape and quality of accuracy are repeated each time
jig	a device manufactured to assist designers and makers to maintain accuracy when repeating the same operation time and again

Batch production

Batch production involves a number of people working on the manufacture of a series of identical products that have been ordered at a specific quantity. Examples include Christmas cakes, T-shirts for a small party, badges, chairs for a restaurant and landing gear for twelve aircraft (A).

Each person has a specific duty to perform. He or she is not solely responsible for the design or manufacture of the complete item, but just a small part or parts of it. There is no likelihood of a repeat order, so a batch production cell can set itself up to manufacture that item alone within its premises for a set amount of time. As workers need not be skilled in every aspect of the production process, they can specialize in certain areas and gradually become better in their specialist fields. The overall quality of the final items therefore remains just as high as one-off items, but at a relative fraction of the cost. **Templates** and **jigs** are used to limit the chances of human error affecting the overall quality of the product when repeat operations are involved.

A comparison between one-off and batch production could be drawn from a boat-building project. One or two people could work together and produce a dinghy from mahogany. They would need to be highly skilled and use many tools and processes to complete the project. At the same time, a team of six to ten equally skilled craftsmen could produce five or six dinghies in the same amount of time by each concentrating on only one small part of the overall process.

A

Aircraft landing gear is batch produced

B

Workers specialize in certain areas

Characteristics of batch production

- There is no need for every worker to be highly skilled in all areas.
- The time taken to produce each item is relatively less than one-off production.
- Templates and jigs are used to maintain high quality.
- Templates and jigs are also used in case a repeat order is required.

Jigs and templates

These will be prepared so that the class can make many identical items without any loss in quality or accuracy. It also limits the opportunities for mistakes. Jigs will be made from wood and metal to prolong their life and resist rough handling in the workshop.

C

D

Fortune teller

You will need to work as a whole class and act as if you are in a company that has just won a contract. You will be working for an imaginary client and you will have to work to deadlines in order to meet their demands.

You will make a simple origami product called a fortune teller (D). To do this, the class needs to be organized into four groups.

- Group 1 will fold and cut the A4 paper into squares.
- Group 2 will fold the fortune tellers into shape and cut out and stick the small coloured squares on the outside leaves of the fortune teller.
- Group 3 will put numbers on the inside leaves.
- Group 4 will write the fortunes on the inside.

Groups 1 and 2 will finish before the others, so should then help group 4 in order to speed up the process.

Tip: Think up ten to fifteen different short fortunes and list them on a sheet of paper, so that you do not have to think up new ones each time.

Think about it!

1. ABC Discuss the differences between one-off production and batch production.
   a) Compare the quality of the design and the quality of the product in the two systems.
   b) How will the designers ensure accuracy?
   c) Who is ultimately responsible for the quality of manufacture in each production method? Which method is more likely to produce a high quality item and why?

Plenary

Batch production is a great way of producing more than one example of the same product. Plans need to be created before an item can be batch produced. What would happen if a plan was not drawn up first?

Producing batches

Jigs and templates

Objectives

In this lesson you will:
- use processes, tools, equipment and techniques with precision
- consider how manufacturing aids are used to ensure accuracy and help volume production.

Key words

template   a shape used by designers to draw around and mark up materials so that the same shape and quality of accuracy are repeated each time

jig   a device manufactured to assist designers and makers to maintain accuracy when repeating the same operation time again

Templates are items that are cut to the exact size of a product and then drawn around (see A). Using a template ensures that no mistakes are made with the marking out of a product and it also speeds up the production process. Templates are made from a range of materials depending on how many times the template will be used and what media is being used with the template. For example, if the template is to be used as a stencil for painting then it will be best to use a thin polystyrene sheet as the template because the plastic is durable and easy to clean. If you need to reproduce the same shape for ten different designs then you could use card for the template.

A **jig** is similar to a template in that it is used to reproduce the same measurements on a product time and time again (see B). For example, in some flat packed bookcases a series of holes are drilled on the inside to put pegs into to support the shelves. These holes need to be drilled in the same place on both sides of the bookcase or the shelves will be uneven. During production a jig is clamped to the sides that has the holes pre-drilled into it. The jig has guides on it so that it can be positioned in the same place on every side. A drill, similar to a pillar drill, is then used to drill the holes using the jig as the guide.

You may have used jigs and templates before in the manufacture of the torch (see pages 58-9). This time, however, the jig will be placed over your work and act as a template and a guide for you to position the holes needed in your design accurately.

The jig will be made from 6mm mild steel or aluminium. You will hold the jig in place using double-sided tape. This avoids the use of clamps that may mark your work. It also saves time. If you do have to use clamps, make sure scrap wood or masking tape is placed on your work to avoid marking or damaging the surface. Several products can be made at the same time by sticking together the centre components on top of each other. All of these will then have the same sizes and dimensions. This technique is found when producing items time and again in small quantities – batch production.

The templates reduce the possibility of human error on the product as all the measuring is contained within the template.

Using a template to ensure accuracy

A

A well-designed jig produced once will allow you to position raw materials many times into such a position to be made quickly and accurately time and again.

Can you identify where a project you have made before could be made successfully by people who are unfamiliar with your design with a series of jigs?

If so, work together and see if you can reproduce it.

Think about it!

123 This is an example of a seven segment display unit

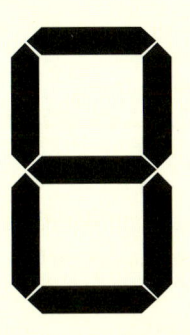

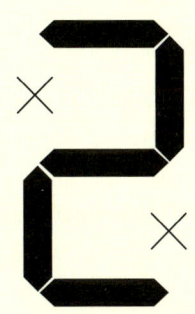

Seven segments are used to make the figure 8. By using only certain 'cells' it is possible to create numbers and letters; for example, covering the top left cell and the bottom right cell produces a figure 2.

Make a seven-segment display template and work out what 'cells' have to be covered to produce the numbers 0–9. Use the template to produce the numbers and underneath write down what cells were covered up. Is there a correlation between the two sets of figures?

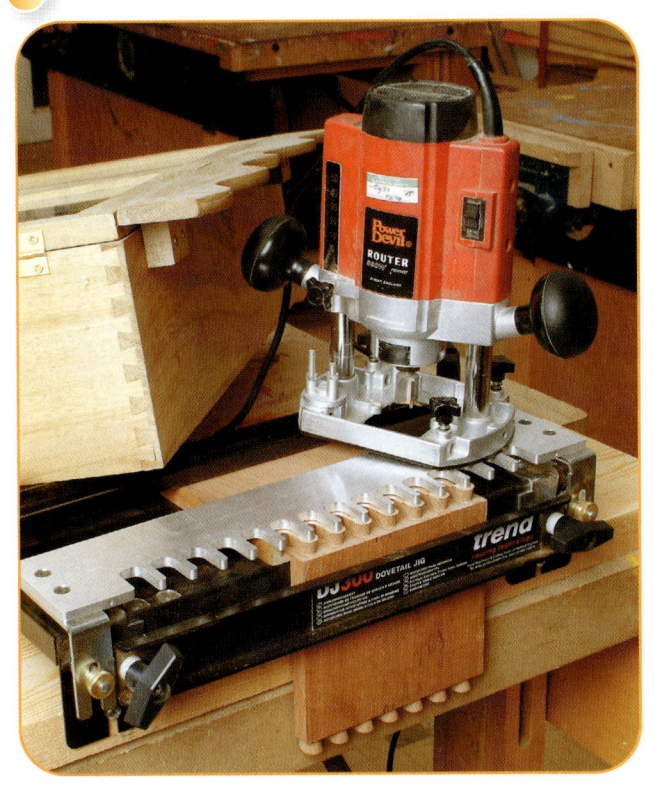

A jig being used in the classroom

Numeracy

When working with jigs and templates you will use the following numeracy skills:

- Tessellation by fitting templates to an area
- Minimizing waste by working out the best way of laying out components in an area
- Calculating the cost of waste material by subtracting waste area from original surface area

When designing for manufacture the use of jigs and templates becomes more obvious. A great deal of materials will be used in production runs where many products are made. The amount of tools and tooling will be greater too.

To make time and again a project that you have made in school would require careful planning. It could be that you identify a series of repeated operations where you needed to measure again and again and check similar dimensions or positions. For example drilling holes opposite each other, or marking out and cutting shapes from stock.

Plenary

Jigs and templates are used to reproduce shapes and measurements to ensure that every product is the same and to provide a quality product. Why is it important that every product in a production run is the same?

Producing batches

Why pencils are yellow!

Objectives

In this lesson you will learn:
- why manufacturers use standard components and sizes to make production easier
- how CAD/CAM can be used to make a batch of identical parts.

Key words

standardized component a common item that is produced in thousands and each one is identical

You will be using pencils as part of your design. As all pencils are the same diameter, you can cut them exactly into short lengths and make **standardized components**. Pencils are an ideal standardized component, as they are colourful, plentiful and easy to use for the design of the product you are going to make.

Designers use standard components (things that already exist) to make production easier. For example, the same buttons can be found on shirts from different manufacturers and cars can use the same bolts, nuts and fixings so repairs and servicing are made easier. Standard components allow manufacturers to concentrate on assembly work rather than making materials from scratch, and this saves time and money.

By using CAD and CAM machines you could manufacture a standard component for use in the classroom on existing projects and products. Designers often find they need to use the same part in many objects – think about bolts, hinges and screws.

You will need to take great care when cutting the pencils using a junior hacksaw or a tenon saw. To avoid splitting the pencil as you cut it, rotate the pencil in your fingers against the bench hook. Repeat this time after time on the backward stroke of

A

the tenon saw. (You can apply this technique when cutting dowell as well.)

A major aspect of your project is using pencils as standard components in order to reduce the number of repeat operations and to speed up production. Before doing this, however, it is worthwhile doing some preliminary research. Exploring the pencil as an investigative exercise enables you to practise the ability to research and find out information.

The history of pencils

Early American pencils were made from Eastern Red Cedar, a strong, splinter-resistant wood that grew in Tennessee and other parts of the south-eastern United States. By the 1900s, pencil manufacturers needed additional sources of wood, and turned to California's Sierra Nevada mountains. There they found Incense-cedar, a species that grew in abundance and made superior pencils. Californian Incense-cedar soon became the wood of choice for domestic and international pencil makers.

B

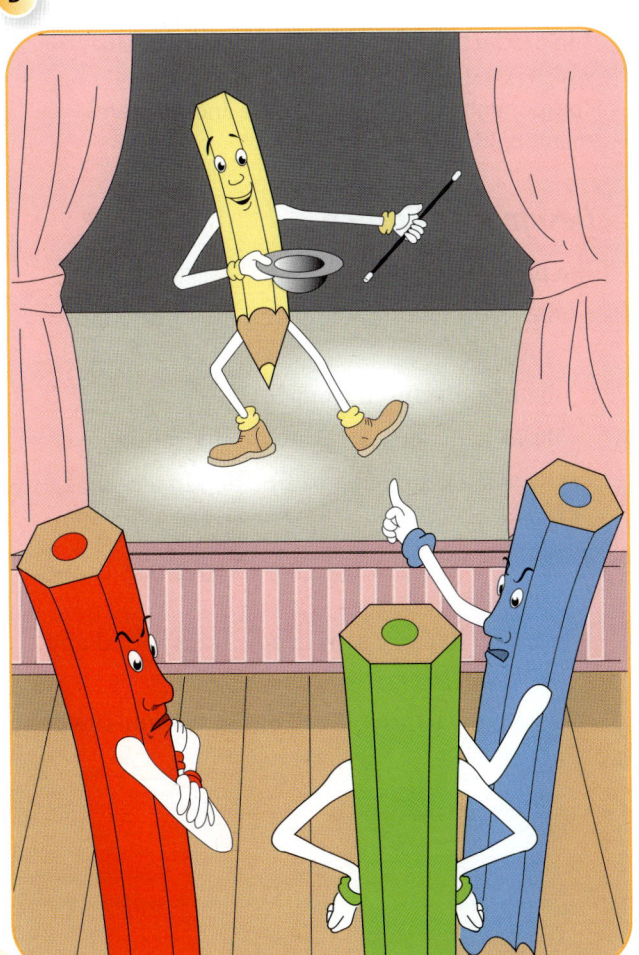

In ancient Rome, scribes wrote on papyrus (an early form of paper) with a thin metal rod called a stylus, which left a light but readable mark. Other early styluses were made of lead. Today we still call the core of a pencil the 'lead' even though it is made from non-toxic graphite.

During the 1800s, the best graphite in the world came from China. American pencil makers wanted a special way to tell people that their pencils contained Chinese graphite, so they began painting their pencils bright yellow. This is because the colour yellow is associated with royalty and respect in China. The American manufacturers believed that painting their pencils yellow communicated this 'regal' feeling and association with China.

Think about it!

Fixtures and fittings such as screws and nails are also standardized components. There are lots of different types of both. Try to find as many different types as you can and carry out these tasks for each one.

a) Draw the component.
b) Write the correct name and size.
c) Note what material it can be used with.
d) What shaped/size screwdriver or hammer would you use on it?
e) What material is it made from?
f) Will it rust?
g) What other tools need to be used to use the component?

Sometimes two pieces of wood need to be joined together but the screw head needs to be hidden, how can this be done?

Plenary

The handles on your kitchen cupboards and drawers are a standardized component. How are they produced so that they are all identical?

Producing batches

The Entertainer

Objectives

In this lesson you will:

- design and make a media storage unit with precision
- choose an appropriate method of making your product
- observe health and safety regulations and control identified risks.

Key words

lay planning   the plan of where to lay out jigs and templates to use the least amount of material and do the least cutting

A   *The Composer*

DMA The Entertainer

The design brief

A pencil manufacturer has recognized that young people use the company's product in all aspects of their schoolwork. It is a familiar product and students often have several sitting in drawers at home or in their pencil cases. The company has also recognized that young people collect music on compact discs. They have designed a product range known as 'The Entertainer', which has the following products:

- The main device is known as 'The Composer' and uses MDF together with half-used pencils. It stores and attractively displays up to ten compact discs.
- 'The Editor' holds 3.5-inch floppy disks and is smaller in scale.
- 'The Director' holds video cassettes.
- 'The Producer' holds DVDs.

The product range focuses on the same theme, which is the use of pencils as a standard component with MDF as a frame and the items that it holds as the decoration.

Design specification

The product will:

- be free standing, requiring no additional support
- be manufactured from MDF
- hold ten compact discs without falling over
- be well decorated and finished in a safe coating
- have a company logo which is clearly displayed
- be easy to carry so it can be transported any where
- be manufactured using jigs and templates

Producing batches

B

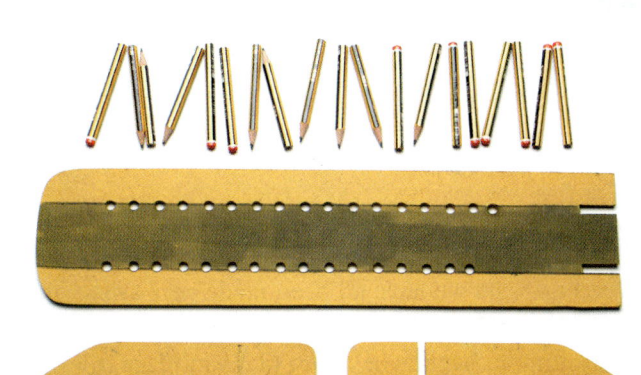

The components used for The Composer

Decide which of the range you are going to produce in groups or as a class activity. You will need to use jigs and templates. You will make the body of the product primarily from one sheet of 10mm MDF. You will need to discuss with your classmates how best to arrange the components in order to minimize waste and lessen the amount of cutting required. This technique and discipline is known as **lay planning**. It is possible to arrange all the different pieces so that there is hardly any waste and the material is used to best effect. Two 'Entertainer' products from the series can be made from one sheet of A4 MDF.

Think about it!

PA Companies often produce a product range, which focuses on the same theme, like the Entertainer. Ford cars, Dyson vacuum cleaners and Crayola drawing products are just some examples.

Pick a popular product range of your choice then carry out these tasks.

a) Draw (or find pictures) and label as many parts of the product range that you can and cut and stick them on a sheet.
b) Why do you think the company has produced a product range?
c) Are there any disadvantages in producing a product range? What are they?
d) Can you think of a suitable method of production for producing more than a thousand, identical items?

Plenary

The next time you go to a craft fair or a traditional toy shop look at the stalls and products for sale and ask yourself how they produce their items so that they are all identical.

B

❶ Using a template

❷ Deciding how to arrange the components

❸ MDF sheet that has been lay planned

85

UNIT 9

Selecting materials

Smart materials and the environment

Objectives

In this lesson you will:
- consider the impact of the material used on the environment
- learn about smart materials
- learn where new materials come from and how they might be used.

Key words

aesthetics how we respond to the visual appearance of a product

smart materials materials that are able to react to the user or the environment such as changes in temperature, moisture, pH or electrical and magnetic fields.

A

In this unit you will make a high-quality product to be presented as a gift. The product is based around a folding structure that sits within a presentation box, which creates an air of mystery as to its contents. Only when the box is opened will the user discover the function of the product! You will need to understand the working characteristics, the production processes, the environmental and social issues and the **aesthetics** of materials, in order to complete this project.

Environment

In recent years we have all been made very aware of environmental issues. Organizations such as the Environment Agency have put plans in place to improve the way we treat the world around us and our quality of life.

The Environment Agency's vision is of a 'rich, healthy and diverse environment for present and future generations'. There are many factors involved in looking after our environment and working towards that vision. We now think more than ever before about the harmful gases and chemicals we put into the atmosphere, things we throw away and what we can recycle, and using the sun, wind and water to make energy.

Many designers are now bringing these ideas into their work. They are trying to minimize environmental damage by selecting materials very carefully and considering the importance of reuse and recycling. Where the product has come from and where it ends up are key questions for a healthy environment.

Think about it!

In groups of five or six, think of a product that you use every day. Answer the following questions and then report back to the class:
- What happens to this product after use?
- How long will it last?
- What might be changed to make it last longer?
- What could be changed to make it last for a shorter time?
- How easily can it be recycled?
- Who will pay the cost of recycling?
- What materials have been used and why?
- Where do the materials come from?
- Are the resources likely to run out?
- Would there be any pollution from this product when it is thrown away or recycled?

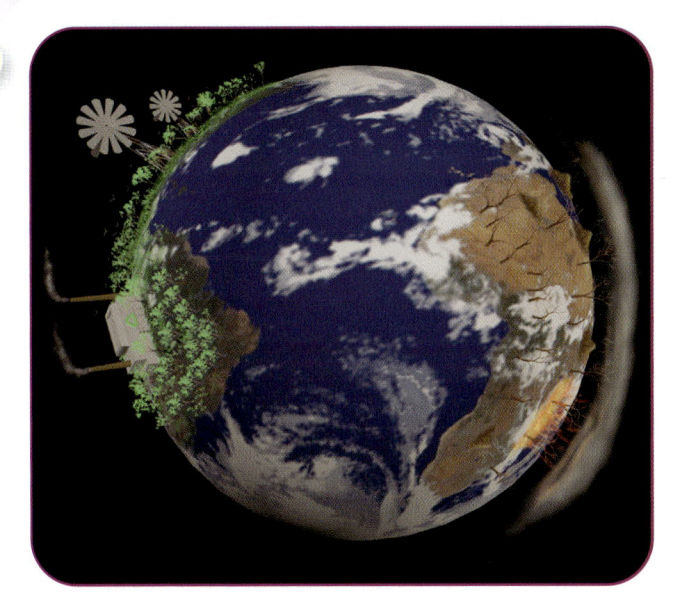

Do designers consider the environment when designing?

Smart materials

A **Smart material** is a family of materials whose physical properties change when they are subjected to different environments (such as temperature or if electric current is applied). Smart materials are being used, and are continually developed, for medical, defensive and industrial products.

Tinted Glass (photo chromic glass) is an example of a smart material. The glass darkens when exposed to light from the visible and ultraviolet spectrum. These are found in sunglasses and visors.

Solar Panels make use of the Photovoltaic cell which captures the power of the sun. Today many items make use of solar panels as their energy source for example hospital power, weather stations, lighting in remote areas (such as decorative garden lamps), radios, buoys and other instances where power is needed short term.

Thermo Ceramics

Thermo Ceramics make it possible to contain certain metals at high temperatures at which they melt. Mixing ceramics and metal powders together to form 'cermets' allows designers to operate machinery at high temperatures that would melt normal alloys and steels.

Shape Memory Alloys (SMART WIRE)

These metals were developed in the 1970's and these alloys can be plastically deformed at certain temperatures. They keep their shape at these temperatures then revert back to their original form. Nickel-titanium and Gold-cadmium alloys are often used in addition to Iron-nickel-cobalt-titanium alloy. The heat is needed to change their shape created by passing electrical current through it. Common wires are 5mm to 5/1000ths of a mm Nitinol has shorter length at 70-80 °C.

Think about it!

ICT For more information on smart materials go to www.heinemann.co.uk/hotlinks and click on this unit. Use the websites or a search engine to find out more about smart materials. How could you use them in your designs? Where are they being used at the moment? How many different types are there? What are they called? How do they work? Are they expensive? If so, why are they expensive?

Think about it!

1. Use a small piece of SMART wire to control a lever and see how far it shrinks and extends in length when voltage is applied.
2. What could it be used for?

Photo chromic paints are made from adding photo chromic pigment to normal paint. When the temperature rises it will force the paint to appear to change colour. These paints are found in products that change temperature for aesthetic and functional purposes. Kettles, car engines and t-shirts make use of such technology.

Paints that contain a phosphorous compound actually gather light energy and can later be seen in the dark. These materials can be applied in the form of paint, but you may have seen it used in toys or glow in the dark stickers.

By using these materials, it will be possible to add that little touch of 'magic' to the projects you are making now and in the future.

Plenary

Many products are given a shelf life. What is a shelf life? How have companies made you aware of what to do with a product once a shelf life has been reached?

Selecting materials

Product analysis: razors

Objectives
In this lesson you will learn about the diversity of one product, the razor, and the influence of lifestyle on products.

Key words
aesthetics	how we respond to the visual appearance of a product
structure	the way something is put together
non-corrosive	a material that will not rust

Look at the two razors shown here (A and B). Consider their characteristics and then have a class discussion.

Man's razor

1. Neutral colour scheme so that it fits into any bathroom décor.

2. It uses two colours so conveying a subliminal message that the two parts need to separate for the operation of the razor.

3. The blade is hidden for safety reasons but also perhaps to indicate that people do not focus on its cold steel appearance.

4. The blade cover is designed as a snap-on fixing – that is, a temporary joint which can be removed time and again without breaking.

5. There is a logo on the most prominent part of the razor, echoing the branding on the packaging, which is the first thing you see at purchase.

6. The overall shape is angular, masculine, functional, instrument-like. Without even knowing what it is, its function could be suggested from its appearance. This is called the science of **aesthetics**.

7. The stem is ribbed to save materials, to provide grip in the wet hand, and to act as a visual 'thinner' and 'lengthener' of the handle. It has shaped edges to increase the comfort in the hand. These characteristics not only make the handle stronger but also save material, as it is a hollow shell **structure**.

Woman's razor

1. The colour is pale blue, which suggests that it is for female use.

2. The shape is slender and shapely rather than a simple handle to support the sharp-bladed head.

3. Similar to the man's razor, the cover is a different colour to the main razor body, suggesting the product is in two parts.

4. The logo is located on the handle as a decorative printing rather than as part of the injected shape.

5. The blade head is smaller than the man's razor.

In both razors, the engineering involved in creating something so delicate, precise and functional that performs well time after time is phenomenal, yet both these items are designed with no expectancy that they are long term. They are disposable razors that cost little to manufacture. The mass production of these items has kept the cost down.

Display and packaging costs are also relatively small, as the way razors are used precludes the need for a permanent storage or display product. This is dissimilar to other items that are associated with grooming, such as more expensive razors, toothbrushes, soap dishes, shower racks and towel rails. The difference is that the disposable razor is easier for the user to throw it away when it reaches the end of its life, rather than continuing with a product that may be unhygienic, inefficient and time consuming to use.

The disposable razor is a classic example of a product that has been designed to satisfy our demands and then be discarded without any guilt when its useful life is over. It is a design classic, as it is instantly recognizable, easy to use, cheap to produce, uses only the materials required for its form and will not date when fashions change. A designer or manufacturer of a century ago would marvel at how such a thing of complexity could be made, used and thrown away within a matter of weeks. Razors are made from cheap and easy to manufacture plastics with steel blades that are sharp and hygienic. In the future, composite materials may allow manufacturers to produce razors as one unit.

Think about it!

1. Identify as many different structures and forces within the razors as possible.
2. Identify the physical requirements of the materials needed to manufacture the razor – for example, they would need to be **non-corrosive**.
3. TS What do you think the designer of the original razor would think about a modern disposable razor?

Think about it!

TS Find three bathroom storage products that have been mass-produced.

a) What changes would have to be made during production if they were to manufactured as one-off products?
b) What would have to be done if these products had to be made from other materials? Think about whether it would be possible and what sort of materials you would use.

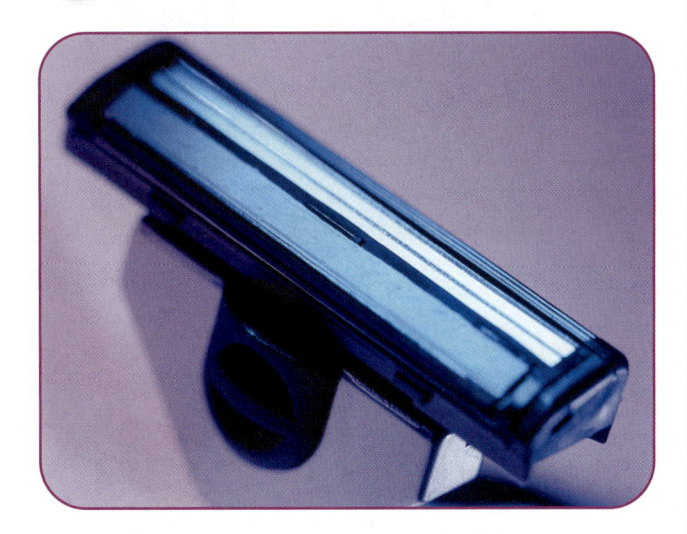

E

Plenary

PA Designers often have to produce a product range that appeals to different gender groups, a good example of this is the razor. Can you think of any other products that have been designed in this way? How have they been designed to do this?

Razor timeline

D

17th	18th	20th	1971	2000+
Hoe type razor		Disposable blade	twin blade razor -disposable	Advanced electronic and disposable razors

Design classics

Objectives

In this lesson you will:
- consider what makes 'good' design
- carry out product analysis on mass-produced items found around the home to identify what makes them successful and **enduring** products.

Key words

| enduring | long lasting |

B

Philippe Starck

A

Richard Powell

C

Charles Rennie Mackintosh

D *Richard Seymour*

Design classics

What is a design classic? This term is often used to describe a product that has a unique or long-lasting appeal. It may be that it is of a particular era or that it is a design so well-thought out that it will be used for years and years.

Many design classics are thought of as very stylish. They are often very simple ideas that have been extremely well put together and are designed to last a long time. They have been tried and tested and proven to work. They have become a part of our daily lives.

Several designers are now famous for producing design classics. Richard Powell (A) and Richard

Seymour (D) are two of the UK's best product designers. Their principles focus on the following:

- the appearance of a product should give visual clues as to what it does and how you use it
- we should continually think of new ways to solve problems
- the product needs an 'x' factor – something that makes you want it
- products are used by humans and that human need should come before technology

Their products include the Duracell Torch, Tefal cordless kettle, Actionman Bike, Minolta Camera, Cyborg Joystick, and Bioform Bra.

Philippe Starck (B) is a French designer who specializes in furniture and is recognized as an expressionist architect. He has decorated the Peninsula Hotel restaurant in Hong Kong and worked on may similar projects in America and London. Starck's designs aim to change the realities of everyday life re-designing everyday items such as the toothbrush, door handles and most famously the lemon squeezer.

Charles Rennie Mackintosh (C) is one of the most celebrated architects and designers of his generation. He emerged in the late 19th and early 20th century and his work focused on natural, symbolic and geometrical elements. His designs are simple and often quirky, and his buildings often came complete with designed schemes of furniture and fittings. One of his most famous works is Glasgow School of Art.

Other design classics

Other design classics include:

- Bic disposable pen
- Austin Mini
- Pritt Stick
- 'Henry' vacuum cleaner
- Raleigh Chopper
- Post It Note
- Concord
- Steam Engine.

All of these were revolutionary when they were designed. They were original concepts that paved they way for future designs.

Plenary

When you are designing try to be as original as possible. Who knows maybe you will be designing the next design classic!

Think about it!

1. **PA** Carry out a product analysis on the contents of a household which are shown in E.
2. **ICT** Go to www.heinemann.co.uk/hotlinks and use the websites to research design classics.
   a) Print off a copy of a famous item and stick it to a sheet of A3 paper. In pairs, annotate the image and identify the materials, the likely production process, the dimensions, and the colour.
   b) Describe the appearance (aesthetics) of the item and make a comment on why it has been identified as a famous design classic.
3. How would the use of SMART materials enhance the everyday items shown in E?

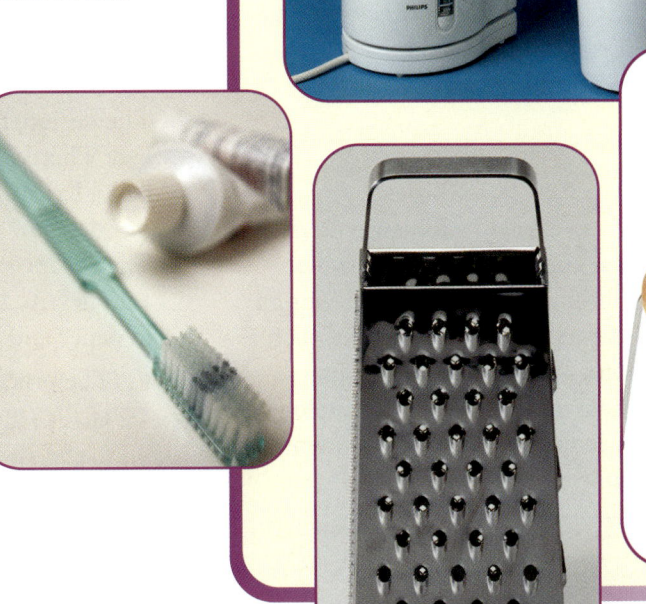

Selecting materials

Product concept model: a case study

Objectives

In this lesson you will:
- look at how a designer gained inspiration for a product
- consider the importance of sketching as part of the designing process
- look at how designers may select materials
- explore different types of smart materials.

Key words

annotation	notes on a design that explain the materials used and how it works
model	3D experiment that designers use to help with their design
prototype	a model or product which has been made to be tested or trialed before being put into production
smart materials	materials that are able to react to the user or environment such as changes in temperature, moisture, pH or electrical or magnetic fields

A

A design story

The design brief was to develop a foldaway item that appealed to both men and women. The designer spent several hours brainstorming a new use for an existing foldaway structure in a new context, such as foldaway chairs, tables and racks. The designer realized that the whole idea of Design Technology is to use existing knowledge to solve new problems and make life easier and/or more enjoyable.

The designer went to the bathroom to get ready for bed. There on the sink sat three disposable razors and a bag of seven razors. This made the designer wonder how to store the razors in a tidy fashion. The razors were the only items that did not 'have a home'. At 10.30 that evening the designer put pen to paper and began sketching.

- The process took only minutes.
- He did not waste time worrying about how it looked.
- He did not rub out his rough drawings to draw them neatly.

92

The design was very rough. The **annotation** involved words that acted as a design specification: razor, storage, attractive, five to ten razors, collapsible, mirror. All these words came from 'using the razor' as an activity. Several sketches were put together. These sketches were the visual recordings of what was in the designer's mind.

The next day, while the design remained in the designer's mind, a **model** was produced using very basic materials, components and construction methods. From this the working **prototype** could be formed, as the design was already 99 per cent recorded.

The essential message of this story is that designing is an activity. The design was captured as it was born and made real in a short time. Sketches helped with this capturing of information. The design could then be communicated with the use of models. The design no longer lived in the head of the designer where it could be lost but was recorded on paper for everyone to use, explore and discuss.

The choice of materials is very important in the designing process. Designers now have even more options with the common use of **smart materials**. Smart materials help designers to consider even more possibilities for their ideas and realise even greater designs.

Smart Materials

A new and exciting example of a smart material in the form of a plastic is Polymorph. Thermoplastics when heated have the ability to change shape, however the temperature has to be very high. Polymorph is made of polymers known as caprolactones, this means that only a fraction of the heat is required to make the plastic pliable enough to mould or shape. You can hold the plastic under hot water set at around 60 degrees and remove it when soft, shape it and leave it to cool. But because it is a thermoplastic the same process can be repeated over and over again. When fully cooled it is very durable and can be sawn, glued or even drilled into.

Polymorph is an ideal mould taking material as it does not make a mess and is safe to use. This is just one example of a whole host of new smart materials that are available today.

Another smart material that can be found in self-adhesive sticker form and in the form of paint is fluorescent pigment. This is a light gathering material that holds the energy taken from light during the daytime. When it is dark it is easy to see the phosphorous giving the appearance that the object is glowing in the dark.

Safety signs, decorations and stickers are sometimes available from stationers (you may have glow in the dark stars at home!). These materials can have a useful application that could save lives too. The pigment is added to signage and gangways on trains, ships and planes so in the event of an emergency and loss of power, the important safety stations and exists can easily be seen.

By combining new materials with existing ones, it is possible to enhance both the performance and the appearance of products. This is something to think about throughout the designing process.

Smart research

See if you can find out about the following smart materials from books or the Internet.
- Tinted glass
- Solar Panels
- Thermo Ceramics
- Shape memory Alloys
- Liquid Crystal Displays (LCD's)
- Piezo-electric actuators

Think about it!

1. Think about what you have designed this year.
2. How did you do it?
3. What will you change from now on in the way you design?

Plenary

It is very important that you put down all of your ideas on paper, that way you will not forget them. Some of the worlds best designs have come from a sudden burst of inspiration that were jotted down quickly so they were not lost.

Selecting materials

Razor sharp

Objectives

In this lesson you will:
- design and make a bathroom storage device that reflects users' needs
- include working characteristics, production processes, environmental and social issues, costs and aesthetics
- use smart materials to improve the function.

Key words

aesthetics — how we respond to the visual appearance of a product

In this unit you will use all of the tips you have learnt about design from Create! to help you produce a product for yourself or someone else, or even an existing company. When you are designing think about form and function and the surroundings that the product will be placed in. Produce a mood board and explore all possible outcomes before committing yourself to a chosen design. Ensure your design is aesthetically pleasing as well as practical. Think carefully about the materials you will select - will they support a folding mechanism, are they recyclable, can modern or smart materials be used in your design?

Think about it!

You may need to research a way of pivoting the mechanisms. Look in a catalogue or visit your local DIY store for information on standardized components for this or try using dowel or small nuts and bolts.

Follow the illustrations and photographs on pages 92-93 to see how the designers' sketches turned into the final items. From these you can design your own device. You can copy directly or design the device and its mechanism from scratch.

Think about it!

You may need to look back at unit 4 pages 26-27 to help design the structure of your bathroom storage device. Think about how products can be designed to distribute forces such as tension, compression and shear.

DMA Razor sharp

The design brief

- To design and manufacture a simple bathroom storage device to hold bathroom items such as razors.

- You have a free choice as to what materials are used to construct the device. You must show that you have considered environmental issues when selecting the materials.
- You have a free choice on how it is decorated and whether such decoration hints at the contents of the device.
- The structure / mechanism of the device will also allow you to hold items other than razors.
- Try and include the use of smart materials - maybe glow paint could be used on the box so that it can always be found in a dark bathroom.

Selecting materials

A

A

Try adding mystery to the storage device too. Does it hold razors, soap, or something else? Could you try and disguise the storage device and make it blend in to a bathroom? Or could you decorate it bright and bold with stripes or dots and make it stand out to entice people's interests and curiosity?

Think about it!

What other items could be held by the storage mechanism?

Plenary

You should now be beginning to find the design process a less daunting task and more of a rewarding one. The design process should be treated as a journey and should be enjoyable. Remember to plan your work thoroughly and use every resource that is available to you.

A prototype example of a folding bathroom storage device.

UNIT 10 Designing for markets

Designing for consumers

Objectives

In this lesson you will consider the importance of consumer needs when designing.

Key words

consumer a person who buys products

Consumer choice

People want choice. They want to choose where to live, what to wear, what music to listen to, what car to drive, what to eat and where to work. The choices people make gives us information about them and tells us how they see themselves.

You need look no further than catalogues, magazines, shop windows, television programmes, car showrooms, music shops, furniture stores and many other shops and services to see the variety of tastes people have and choices they make. You will also be able to see what is new, fashionable and popular, and how quickly people's needs and desires change. Sometimes things come back into fashion; the same themes of colour, shape and texture are used time after time.

Think about it!

Think about your own bedroom. There are many ways in which your bedroom could be decorated, but you have chosen one particular style. You have also chosen many of its contents and how it is laid out. What does your bedroom say about you?

Designing for consumers

As a designer, you have the responsibility of creating new, innovative products or reshaping existing objects to enhance the quality of people's lives. You must also make sure that you are designing products that people will want to use. Good design is about balancing the function of a product with its form. The product you are making in this project should be regarded as an item that will contribute to the quality of routine life, in the same way that the pen, the T-shirt, the car, the desk lamp and the bottle opener do.

Your design should be able to contribute to routine life in the same way as these items

A *Alessi*

Designing for markets

Quality is something that all consumers now demand in all goods and services regardless of the price they have paid. We expect a quality item as we naturally assume that machines are involved at nearly every stage in production and as a result reduce the opportunity for things to go wrong during manufacture resulting in products that may not fit, run erratically or fail to work after a short period of time.

B

Namiki house

C

Plenary

As a designer you have to be aware of new designs and materials so that your designs can be up to date and fresh. Read technology books and magazines, browse the Internet regularly and watch technology based television programs to keep your knowledge fresh and modern.

Designing for markets

Market research

Objectives

In this lesson you will:
- learn how manufacturers generate and develop new ideas for products
- design a questionnaire to find out about the market needs for your product.

Key words

market research	the method of finding out what people like and need in a product
open-ended question	a question with many possible answers and responses
closed question	a question with only a limited number of possible answers

Designers and manufacturers often test their ideas before they commit to full-scale production by producing a prototype design. This could be a full size replica or concept model of the final item for consumers to touch and handle and get the 'feel' of. This process of 'realization' of the design helps designers and manufacturers discuss the product with potential consumers and so raise the overall quality of the finished product. In so doing, designers can assess the likely reaction of consumers and potential end users for the future and determine how well their idea will meet expectations. This is an important part of market research and can be used as part of a questionnaire.

Surveys and questionnaires are used by designers and **market researchers** to canvas a response from people in order to find out what products are likely to sell successfully. Questionnaires can also be used to find out what fashions are popular and how people feel about things. Overall they produce various data about society and indicate trends that may be useful to designers.

The design and implementation of a survey can greatly affect the results obtained by those carrying out the research. Research methods are a branch of science in itself but there are some basic rules that apply to most data collections (see B).

Open-ended and closed questions

Take care with the use of **open-ended** and **closed questions**. This is an example of an open-ended question.

'What woods will you use for your project and why?'

This is an example of a closed question.

'Which of the following woods will you use for your project?'

Mahogany	☐
Teak	☐
Pine	☐
Sycamore	☐

The development of the consumer society

In the 1950's products were advertised and marketed based on how they performed. Manufacturers emphasised the product name and how it performed as the major selling point of mass products.

A

Designing for markets

B

- When writing a survey, remember you are trying to extract information about the likes and dislikes of your end user.
- You need to use the information to help you with your designs.
- Do not be disheartened if you do not get the answers you were expecting.
- The questions should be easy to understand and answer.
- Do not expect your client to take ages answering your questions.
- Provide tick boxes and areas for answers.
- Ensure the questions flow in a relevant order.
- You should ensure that your questions look neat on the page and have no spelling mistakes.
- Sometimes it is a good idea to allow people to tick a scale of response rather than closed questions as strength of feelings can then be measured.

However it was feared that supply would outstretch demand as people bought well made products that were built to last. Because of this designers and manufacturers began to make products that looked different each year, suggesting there was something inferior about the previous model or design so that public demand remained strong for new products.

In the 1960's people began to feel the need to express themselves as individuals which they did through the objects they purchased. Manufacturers had to develop products that allowed people to express themselves individually and thus the mass production of identical items became more flexible and allowed for more variety.

Focus groups were in the late 60's and early 70's. Here people were asked about what unconscious motivations caused them to buy certain products at certain times. Focus groups are still used today and along with questionnaires form the basis of all market research which allows designers to greaten the chance of producing products that will sell more successfully in the future.

Plenary

Collecting research before commencing any design work is very important but make sure you are collecting relevant information and not just asking questions for the sake of asking questions. Also try to get the opinions of a wide range of people and not just the people you know.

Think about it!

Conduct a survey to find out how candles are used in and around people's houses and then use this information to help with your designs.

Name............................Gender M ☐ F ☐

1) Do you have candles in your home?   Yes ☐   No ☐
2) Are they ever lit?   Yes ☐   No ☐
3) Are the candles on a stand or mat?   Stand ☐   Mat ☐   Neither ☐
4) How much would you pay for a stand for a candle? _____
5) Where are candles mainly used in your house? _____
6) What material would you prefer a candleholder to be made from?
   Wood ☐
   Metal ☐
   Plastic ☐
   Other ☐
7) Who would you buy a candleholder for? _____

Designing for markets

Quality assurance

Objectives

In this lesson you will:
- learn about designing for manufacture
- learn about the main commercial processes that are used by manufacturers
- consider how ICT influences manufacturing in industry
- learn how quality assurance systems are used during the design stage to plan safe and accurate production
- learn about tolerances.

Key words

quality control	checking that the quality has not dropped during manufacture
tolerance	the amount of difference that is acceptable between two products that are said to be identical

The main aim of this unit is for you to learn about the processes used by manufacturers when designing and manufacturing a product for the market place. The product you will make will be made to the same quality and high standard of finish as you would expect to find in a high street store. You will use the skills and knowledge you obtained from the Spot on! project where you were engaged in manufacturing in quantities.

A

Quality control is an important part of industry

Quality

Ensuring quality is part of the designing process. Quality means making sure that the right product is designed at the right time to meet the needs of people who want it. Many large companies invest large sums of money and much time to ensure that they provide goods and services to the highest quality throughout every stage of the design and manufacturing process. Good quality assurance is only achieved where there is a constant communication between the designers and the consumers. In other words, a good client and designer relationship will result in a well-made product that lasts.

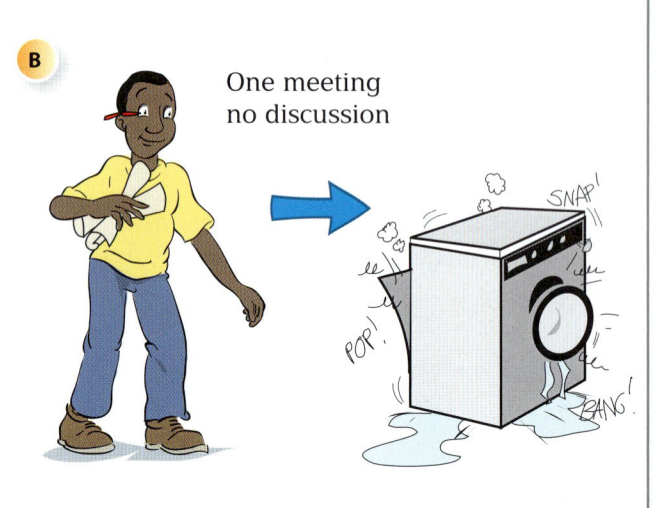

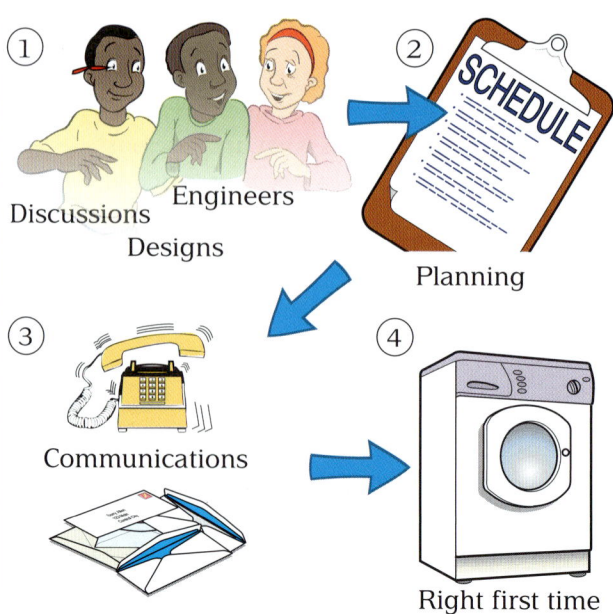

B

One meeting no discussion

① Discussions Designs Engineers

② Planning

③ Communications

④ Right first time

Designing for markets

One branch of quality assurance is the discipline of **quality control**. Quality control involves the regular monitoring, measurement and inspection of designs and manufacturing stages throughout the design and manufacturing process to ensure that goods are well within specific **tolerances**. Quality control can involve anything from the checking of drawings to the inspection of cutting tools on a machine. Quality assurance concerns itself with how these systems are monitored and associated with the overall operation of a company.

Quality assurance and consumers

Quality is something that all consumers now demand in all goods and services regardless of the price they have paid. We expect a quality item as we naturally assume that machines are involved at nearly every stage in production and as a result reduce the opportunity for things to go wrong during manufacture resulting in products that may not fit, run erratically or fail to work after a short period of time. ICT is used in manufacturing to ensure accuracy and quality products.

Tolerances

Tolerances are the small acceptable errors that are created when products are made time and again. Products differ in size by small distances or depths but these usually do not affect the overall operation or performance of a product. Any differences can only be greater or smaller than the specific requirements by a small percentage. An example of this is a resistor where the coloured bands around its circumference indicate that the value of its resistance can be + or – 5%. In other words, a 100 ohm resistor could be either 105 or 95 ohms in value. It is too difficult to manufacture them many times and still to have exactly the same value; the methods in which they are made cannot guarantee this level of accuracy.

Quality control plan

Complete a quality control table during the manufacture of your projects and indicate where you need to discuss ideas and processes with your teacher.

If a company meets a certain recognized standard of quality provision and control procedures, it is awarded with ISO 9000 series of quality certification.

Think about it!

1. **ICT** Look up ISO on the Internet.
   a) Find out about the different ISO standards.
   b) Find out how often companies are inspected to meet their quality provision status.
2. **ABC** Now that you have been introduced to the theory of quality, write a plan on how you would ensure that the products in table C are made to a high standard.

C

	Who are you going to source for information?	What questions should you ask?	Why?	What action can you take now?
Allsorts				
Mars bar				
Bird box				
Desk lamp				
Chair				
Calculator				

3. **TS** Think of all the ways ICT is used in the manufacturing industry. How has ICT changed methods of quality control?
4. **ICT** Use the Internet to research the history of manufacturing. How has manufacturing changed over time?

Think about it!

When you are designing your own work, think of the opportunities for things to go wrong and how during the design and the manufacturing process you can limit these errors by being pro-active and identifying these possible events occurring.

Plenary

Remember that you are designing and making products that will be used by other people. Make sure that you carry out thorough and detailed checks throughout your projects so that the outcome will be high quality.

Designing for markets

Flow charts

Objectives

In this lesson you will learn about the use of flow charts.

Key words

flow chart   a chart using symbols to show the sequence of a process

pictorial flow chart   a flow chart using very few words

To ensure that your product is high enough quality for consumers it is important that you plan the production.

You need to create a map in your mind about the different stages you need to go through before starting, for example, the simple process of cutting a piece of pine using a tenon saw can be split into the following stages;

- collect together the pine, a pencil, try square, glass paper, bench hook and tenon saw
- decide where the cut line should go
- using the pencil and square mark the cut line on the pine
- hold the pine on the bench hook with one hand and cut using the tenon saw with the other
- remove any splinters using the glass paper.

The same detail is needed to plan larger projects, **flow charts** are often used to help with this.

You may have used flow charts before to plan your work. Flow charts are helpful because they enable you to see at a glance what work you are doing and what you can look forward to achieving. Diagram A shows some useful flow chart shapes that have been given British Standard status. A British Standard means that wherever these symbols are used, all designers understand the same information. This ensures the same level of quality throughout the design and manufacturing process.

Use the example shown in unit 7, page 60 as a basis for your project planning. Remember that there are going to be many small operations within the manufacturing process of your project as there are lots of different parts to be cut and shaped in different ways. You can mention jigs and templates in the manufacturing plan as these devices improve the overall quality of the product.

Include an estimation of time and any health and safety points on the chart. This will help you or the manufacturer to see how long the project will take to produce and what safety precautions need to be taken.

A

This is used to show part of a process (orange)

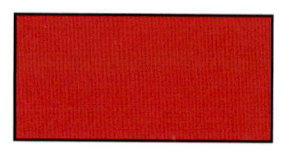

Preparation: this represents the beginning or end of a process (red or green)

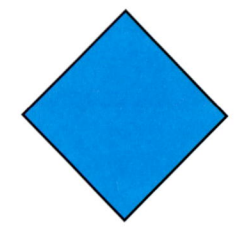

This indicates that a decision has to be made and that it could lead to other processes or parts in the manufacturing (blue)

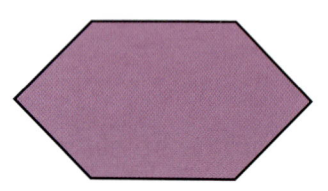

This indicates a delay, a halt or an interruption in the process, such as waiting for glue to dry (purple)

102

Designing for markets

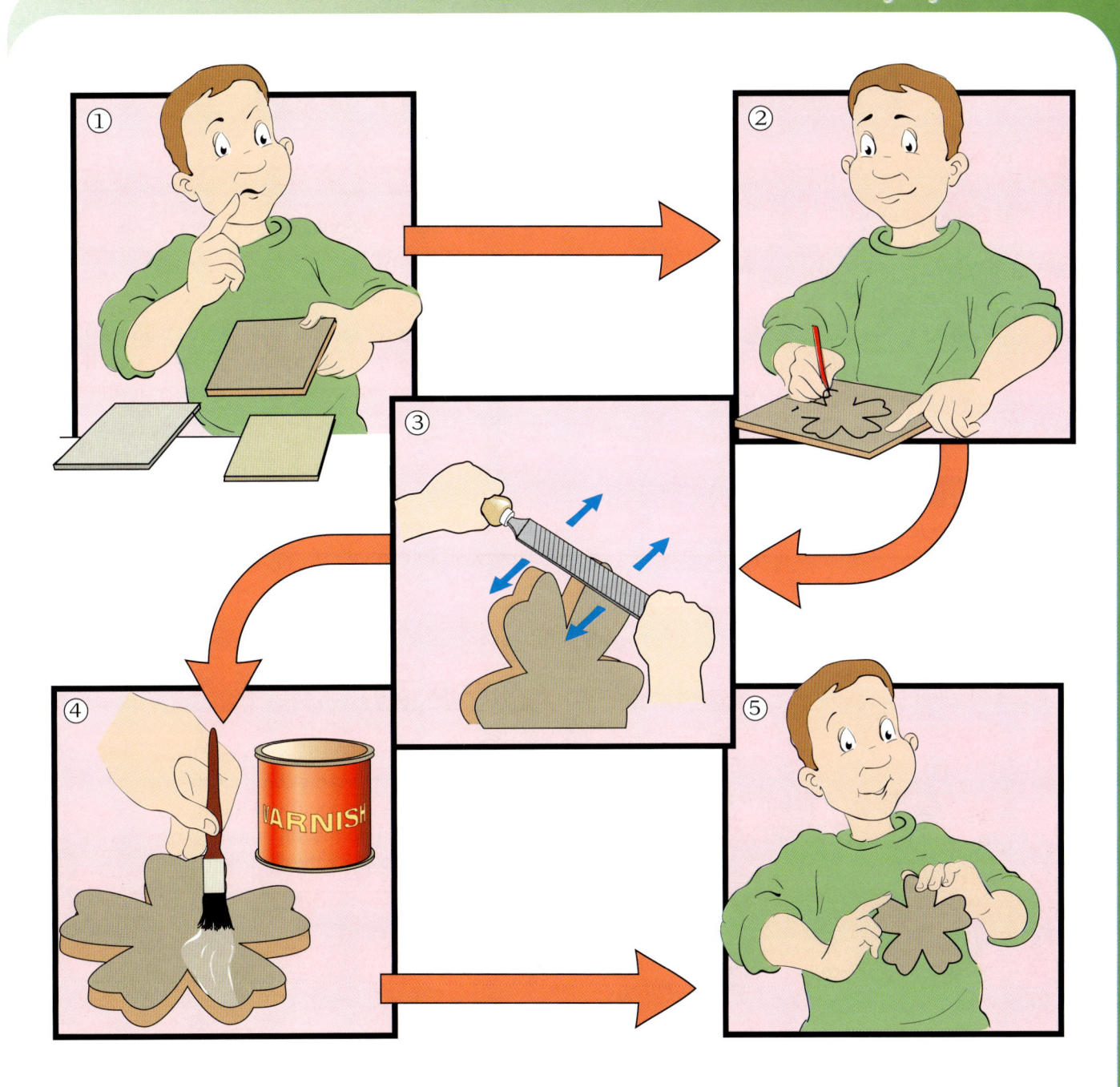

Pictorial flow charts

You could also present the production process as a series of pictures. This is known as a **pictorial flow chart**. This method is useful for anyone with no technical understanding to follow what you did step by step. Pictorial flow charts use very few words so that people can see the process almost entirely through the illustrations you have drawn. Pictorial flow charts consist of linked boxes containing simple line pictures of activities being undertaken.

Think about it!

Produce a flowchart to show the production of the fortune teller from page 78-9.

Plenary

Plans of work are very useful to refer back to and are often used by other people who need to recreate your design. You must check that your plan works well so that someone else can follow it and create the same design.

Designing for markets

Production for profit

Objectives

In this lesson you will:
- learn about spreadsheets which can help with costing and scaling up
- understand the term 'marketing' and the concept of 'profit and loss'
- develop an awareness of the tensions between human development and welfare.

Key words

product lifecycle   the changing sales of a product during its time on the market

Product lifecycle

A shows a **product lifecycle**.

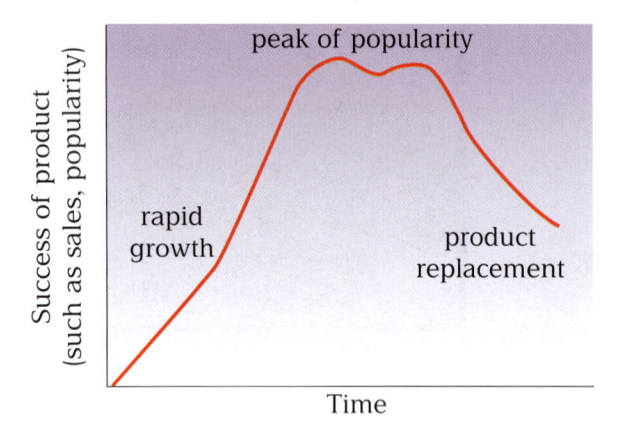

A

[Graph showing Success of product (such as sales, popularity) on y-axis versus Time on x-axis. Curve shows rapid growth rising to peak of popularity, then declining to product replacement. X-axis label: Period product is available to the public]

At first products sell rapidly and popularity spreads quickly because it is either a new idea or something that may be fashionable.

After a period of time, this initial burst tails off as the product matures. Sometimes sales are boosted by a different version or a new model with slight changes or a clever advertising campaign. This period of sales depends on the feedback the designers

Think about it!

In pairs, list five popular products that are new and original and have only launched very recently.

and manufactures receive from people who have purchased and used the product and how well they think it operates to make improvements in the future.

The product will then start to fall in sales as its popularity becomes stale. People grow tired of it or a new product that does the same job better is launched. Eventually the product sales stop and that particular model is no longer available.

This is true for all products from cereals to motor cars.

Think about it!

ICT Research and look up a 'family' or brand of products from the same company that have been launched time and again. Use the Internet to help you search for information on your chosen brand. Produce a display for the classroom wall.

KitKat has a large family of products

This product lifecycle helps to develop a designers ideas to create better products that perform to a higher standard each time.

Designing for markets

Marketing

Marketing is an essential part of keeping this cycle in motion. It is the science of discovering peoples' behaviour and using this to sell products time and again. Advertising, research and consumer groups are all part of the marketing process: without successful marketing products would fail to sell to the right people at the right time and therefore fail to make profits for manufacturers.

You may have seen people collecting information in the street by asking questions, or you may have received direct mail questionnaires through the post or in magazines. You may have even given your personal details when you have bought something in a store. All these processes collect information that is held by consumer groups to target specific consumers with products that may appeal to them.

Think about it!

TS Find out what the Data Protection Act is and what Statutory Rights are. Find out what the Consumers Act is and how all these affect you, your purchasing power and your rights as a consumer.

Marketing can cost a lot of money and time. The revenue for marketing is created in a number of ways through investors and shareholders or by using the profits made on the last sales of a product.

Profit and loss

Profit is the money (capital) that is left after all the costs have been subtracted from the money gathered from the total sales of a product. Imagine you sold your school projects in a class for £200. If it cost £50 in materials, £30 in resources, energy and labour, electricity, room hire, rent, insurance and so on (all these are known as overheads), £40 in advertising the product, £10 to find out whether it would sell in the first place (marketing) and finally £40 to pay back your teacher (shareholder or board of directors who gave you a loan) then you would be left with a profit of £30. This could then be either divided amongst everyone in the class, invested in other markets, or used to develop a new product range.

Spreadsheets help you keep track of your incoming and outgoing money and where money is being spent. It is a legal requirement for companies to keep their 'books' in order and to pay the correct taxes, rates and levys during the production process.

Projects run at a loss when the total sales fail to pay off the overhead costs and you are left with excess products or low sales that fail to bring in more revenue.

The complex economic world of money investment, shareholding, marketing, advertising and consumer monitoring means the designer needs to create products that sell in order that manufacturing companies can survive.

Think about it!

ICT Find out what the FTSE is. What are stocks and shares? What is the G7? What are bluechip and high risk companies?

Choose a company and track its economic performance over a period of time as a class activity and find out who performs better over a six week period.

Plenary

Niche market products

PA Look at one of the following items: spaghetti tins, mobile phones, rucksack.

ABC Write down:
- its special features
- what makes the product unique or new
- who the is product aimed at.

Designing for markets

Just-in-time production

Objectives

In this lesson you will:
- learn about just-in-time production
- find out when this method is appropriate to use in manufacture.

Key words

just-in-time (JIT) production	stock control in industry which involves designing and making in response to demand
assets	useful or valuable items such as materials

The use of computers has increased the speed and accuracy with which products can be made. The characteristics of CAD/CAM systems are that products can be made in a relatively short time to a cost effective strategy, with limited errors and inaccuracies. Mass production methods rely on a huge investment in high-quality machining and computer technologies. The initial investment in these assembly lines is immense and companies need to be sure that whatever they make will sell quickly and go on selling for some time while production is in process.

Examples of mass-produced objects include mobile phones, cars, televisions, trainers, sweets, calculators, pencils and tennis balls. All these items are produced in vast quantities and can be bought for a relatively low cost. It is the number of items bought that brings in revenue for companies involved in the production of these items.

Relative low cost is an important term. The investment in setting up a factory and fitting it out with complex machinery and resources, designing the way it operates and its staffing and infrastructure will cost hundreds and thousands and sometimes millions of pounds before a single item is produced. However, when the production process starts and thousands of items are guaranteed to be sold each week, the money invested will be returned to the company. Pens, phones and cars, cost little to manufacture compared to how much money will be made from selling them.

A *Examples of mass produced products: mobile phones and sweets*

Designing for markets

Just-in-time production involves the delivery of materials or designs in response to customer demands. For example, a red sports car with cream seats made to order will begin with the customer making the order and then the company will source the materials from different areas rather than from their own stock. The JIT method of manufacture aims to reduce the amount of stock that stays within a company's **assets** at all times.

Jaguar, for example, mass produces luxury motor vehicles. However, their products can still be made to order by allowing the potential customer to stipulate the extras, fittings, engine performance and colour schemes before production commences.

Think about it!

PA Mind map some items from around the home and school and discuss how they are made.

- If they were originally mass produced, think about what would have to be changed in order for them to be made by hand.
- What would have to be changed if they were originally made by hand and now had to be produced in their thousands.

See if you can identify the key features of mass production in terms of labour, quality, costs, time and environmental impact.

Plenary

Time yourself individually on how long it takes to sharpen five pencils by using a hand pencil sharpener.

Then time five people doing the same activity with one pencil each and finally one person operating a electronic sharper or more effective desk mounted sharpener.

What manufacturing style do they each represent?

Now can you envisage the same issues for other products you are familiar with?

This item is likely to be a 'one off' and therefore very expensive to produce!

Designing for markets

Light my fire!

Objectives

In this lesson you will work successfully as a team to design for high-volume manufacturing.

Key words

aluminium	a light silver coloured metal
JIT Just in Time production	designing and making in response to consumer demands
CAD	Computer Aided Design
CAM	Computer Aided Manufacture
risk	the likelihood that a hazard will occur

This unit requires you to work closely as a team. Think back to your work in unit 8 pages 78–79.

DMA Light my fire!

The design brief

To design and manufacture a small tea light/nightlight holder from **aluminium** sheets, acrylic or MDF.

Wherever possible in this project use **JIT** production and **CAD/CAM** facilities to manufacture the design and questionnaires to canvas opinion about how the design can be personalized and how the package can be marketed and sold. 6mm acrylic, MDF or aluminium, or even a combination of all three materials, can provide ideal materials for the holder. Packaging the product is an important part of production. You may wish to think of a name, company logo, safety instructions and safe operation information for the buyer as part of the final packaging.

Useful dimensions: a tea light is 40mm in diameter, and a little under 20mm in height (A).

The safety issues of the project need to be explored and a **risk** assessment should be carried out to find a suitable surface finish for the product.

Design specification

The tea light holder needs to:

- pack flat
- be made of three pieces of material only
- be packaged if possible to enhance chances of selling to potential end users
- make use of jigs and templates in its production
- hold one tea light safely and securely

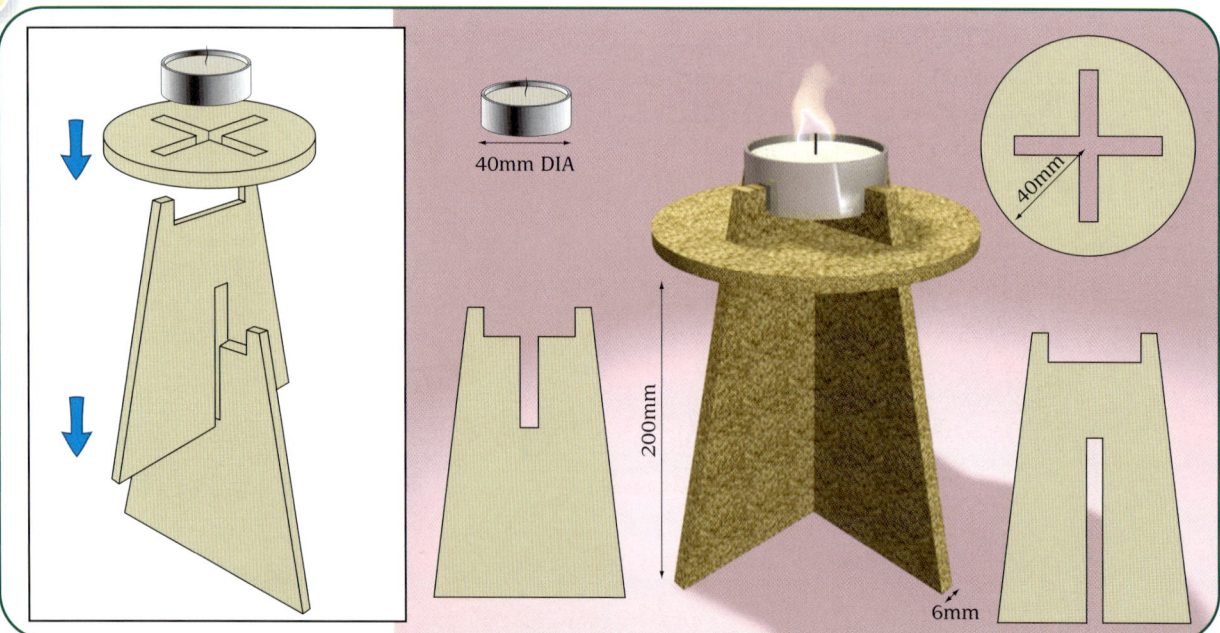

A

Designing for markets

Fire resistant materials

You are going to be producing a tea light/night light holder so it is important that you design your product with safety in mind. Whatever material you decide to use will have to be resistant to fire. Quality control and risk assessment checks will have to be done at the initial stages of production.

When using wood that will be in close proximity to fire there are several things that can be done to help make it safe. The wood can be treated with a fire retardant spray or lacquer or a fire retardant variety of paint or varnish (read the label on the tin to check that it is fire retardant). Hard woods are more resistant to heat than softwoods and some varieties of manufactured board are produced with a fire retardant ingredient in them.

Metal has a higher resistance to heat and is less likely to catch fire, however if you are planning on painting your holder read the label before choosing which to use.

Plastic is the most likely material to be affected by heat. Use a plastic that has a high melting point such as acrylic rather than using polystyrene.

If there is an opportunity in your school to cast aluminum then ask if you can do so. A successful candleholder can be made from casting a polystyrene pattern in sand. Shape the block of polystyrene to the style you wish and then with the assistance of your teacher you can bury this pattern in casting sand (use *petribond* or green sand). Make sure there is an entry hole (runner) and an exit hole (riser) for the gases, hot metal can then be poured into the mould and burn away the polystyrene leaving a metal version to cool in the mould overnight.

Knocking away the sand reveals the casting that can be later filed and polished to make a more solid and impressive candleholder.

Think about it!

D Once you have constructed your tea light/night light holder investigate the possibility of adding fabric or rubber to the feet. These materials can be purchased with a self-adhesive back so there is no need for glue. This will prevent your holder from scratching any surface it is placed on.

Packaging your product can also improve the sale potential. A well-presented box with information about the product will help to promote the quality of the product inside. Produce a box for your holder using coloured card rather than white. Use a computer to produce the words and graphics.

Plenary

When designing it is important to think about every detail, no matter how small as this improves the overall quality of the product. Remember to ask yourself the question, 'Would I buy this product?' If the answer is no then you need to improve it.

Think about it!

1 TS You have worked in a team during the production of your tea light night light holder. Think about how companies are made up of teams to ensure quality manufacture.

   Tip! Look back at your work in this unit.

2 TS Is teamwork still as important in one-off production?

UNIT 11 Using control for electronic monitoring

Introducing radios

Objectives
In this lesson you will discover how important radio communication is in our lives.

Key words
circuit — an unbroken flow of electrical current
signal — a wave of sound that transmits information

History of radio communications

Heinrich Hertz was the first to discover electro-magnetic waves in 1887 but it was not until 1897 that Guglielmo Marconi realized the commercial potential of radio. He made popular the method of wireless communication and paved the way for morse code to be transmitted over the airwaves.

The first radios available for popular use were called 'crystal sets'. These radios were relatively inexpensive for people and allowed the first family of listeners to catch up on news, stories and social information. Public broadcasting soon took off as people could now listen to live news and music whilst at home. Many early listeners built their own crystal radios, such was the demand for people to hear events as they happened. What made radio even more popular was that anyone could access it.

The manufacturers of the early radios assisted the rapid development of public broadcasting when they asked the government to let them establish radio stations. The end result was the formation of a broadcasting company, in 1922 – the BBC.

Valves allowed manufacturers to design and build more powerful radios. The valve allowed a higher output from the circuitry, which meant speakers could be added into radios so that groups of people could all listen in at any one time. As listening to the radio became a social event for families and friends, it was not uncommon for the radio to be found at the centre of a room. Early radios were designed to look like pieces of furniture and so they tended to blend in to their surroundings rather than look like technical equipment, as they do today.

Transistor radios

Although some enthusiasts and high fidelity equipment still use valves, the transistor invented in 1947, at Bell Telephone Laboratories, revolutionized radio performance. The Regency TR-1 was the first transistor radio available in 1954 and cost approximately £30. From then transistor and silicon technology allowed radios to become smaller, cheaper to produce and their sound quality and versatility improved all the time.

The next revolution is already changing the way in which we listen to our music, news and entertainment. Digital technology offers us an even higher quality information and wider range of programmes to suit our tastes.

A *Trevor Bayliss and the wind up radio*

The main aim of this project is for you to make use of existing electronic circuitry and components to produce a useful and exciting product for teenagers. You will bring together all the aspects of designing and manufacturing you have learned in order to complete a fully operational, high quality personal AM radio. There are many radios currently on the market, but you have to design within a budget. Each item on a 'bill of materials' will be priced.

Throughout the project each part, component or consumable material will have a price attached to it. It is up to you to either match your abilities and skills to accomplish what you can do yourself or to buy in components and skills. This will introduce you to the basics of contracting, economics, and money and materials management.

B

C

D

Radios are still changing and can be found in many forms

Circuit systems

The arrangement of the components in your **circuit** and the special functions that they carry out allows you to build a device that successfully decodes radio waves. Radio waves are around us all the time, which is why a radio should work anywhere in the world. More complex receivers can distinguish between all the frequencies and radio stations and process them so as they are clear and of high quality. However, the circuit you use in this project will allow you to pick up information from radio stations that are broadcasting along the Amplitude Modulation Band.

In earlier projects the systems approach was used to split up a process into small parts. Here, the same method is used in the following way. The radio is basically made of input parts that receive and locate a radio **signal**. This is then passed to a process part of the circuit that separates the signal from other interfering signals. Finally the radio signal is sent to an output stage. This amplifies the signal (makes it bigger) by utilizing a device such as a speaker so that the listener hears the sound.

Think about it!

1. **ICT** Go to www.heinemann.co.uk/hotlinks and click on this unit to research Trevor Bayliss. What did he invent?
   Why was his design so special?
2. **ICT** Explore the BBC site and listen to the radio live over the web. What can you discover about the programmes.

FPT Radio disassembly

Take apart some radios in the classroom and see how they are assembled and held together. Can you spot the systems used in their operation and how they work?

Plenary

Try to think about what life would be like without radio waves. How would the emergency services, the armed forces or travel industries function?

Using control for electronic monitoring

Your circuit board

Objectives

In this lesson you will explore what makes a successful printed circuit board (PCB).

Key words

printed circuit board (PCB) a circuit formed by printing or soldering the circuit onto a surface instead of using wires

Diagram A shows an example of the circuit you will be using. There are other types of circuit; your teacher may have circuits that behave differently. This particular circuit can be used to copy from and then change into 'tracks' that could be used to produce **printed circuit boards (PCBs)**.

You will use the following components:
- integrated circuit MK484
- transistor BC548B
- 150pF variable tuning capacitor
- ferrite rod
- 2.5 metres of 0.0315 diameter enamelled copper wire
- ×2 100K resistors (brown/black/yellow) – remember to use the resistor colour code to check this
- ×2 1K resistors (brown/black/red)
- ×1 270R resistor (red/violet/brown)
- ultra-miniature slide switch (you may wish to use a different method or switch)
- ×2 100 nF capacitors
- ×1 10 nF capacitor
- ×1 47uF capacitor
- ×1 head phone circuit
- ×1 AA battery holder
- insulation tape, wire, solder, screws as required to attach board to device that you design.

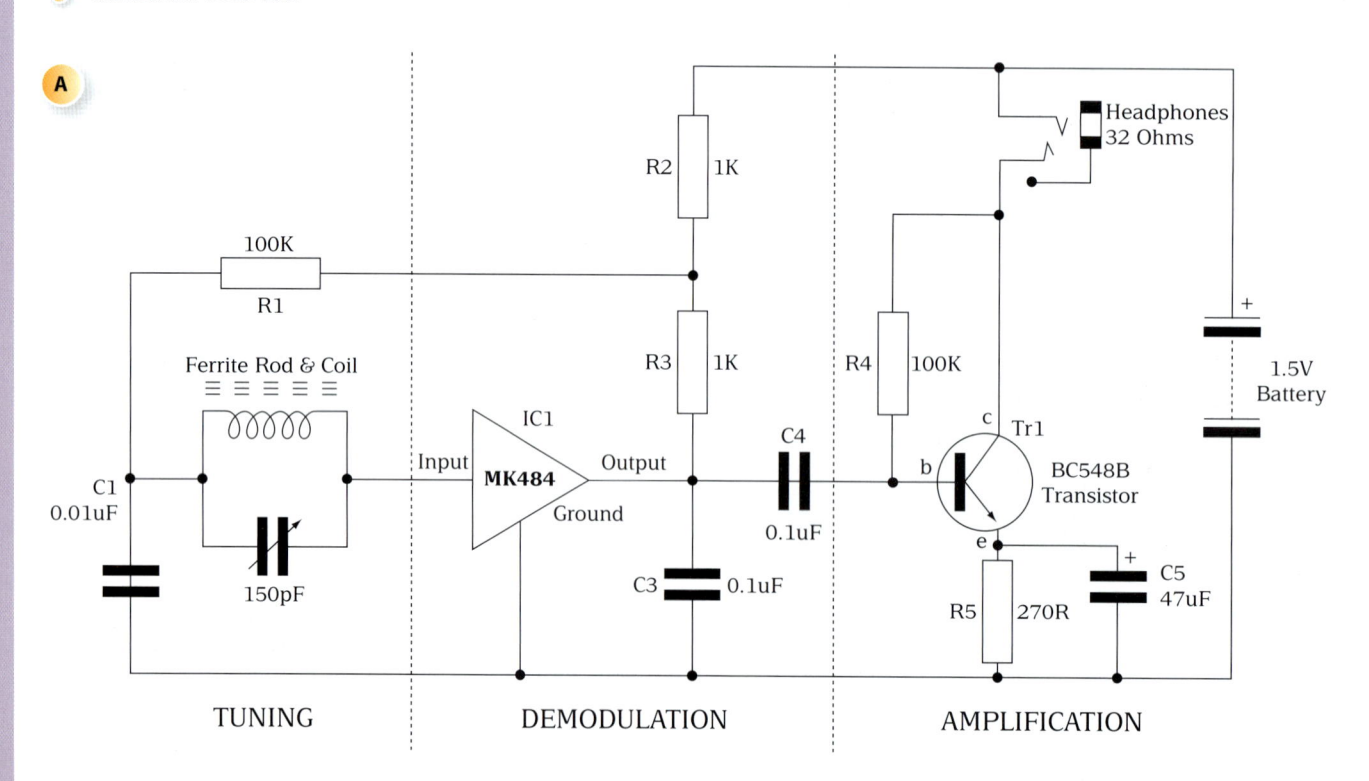

A

[Circuit diagram showing TUNING section (C1 0.01uF, Ferrite Rod & Coil, 150pF variable capacitor, R1 100K), DEMODULATION section (IC1 MK484 with Input, Output, Ground; R2 1K, R3 1K, C3 0.1uF, C4 0.1uF), and AMPLIFICATION section (R4 100K, Tr1 BC548B Transistor, R5 270R, C5 47uF, Headphones 32 Ohms, 1.5V Battery)]

Printed circuit board of a radio

Using control for electronic monitoring

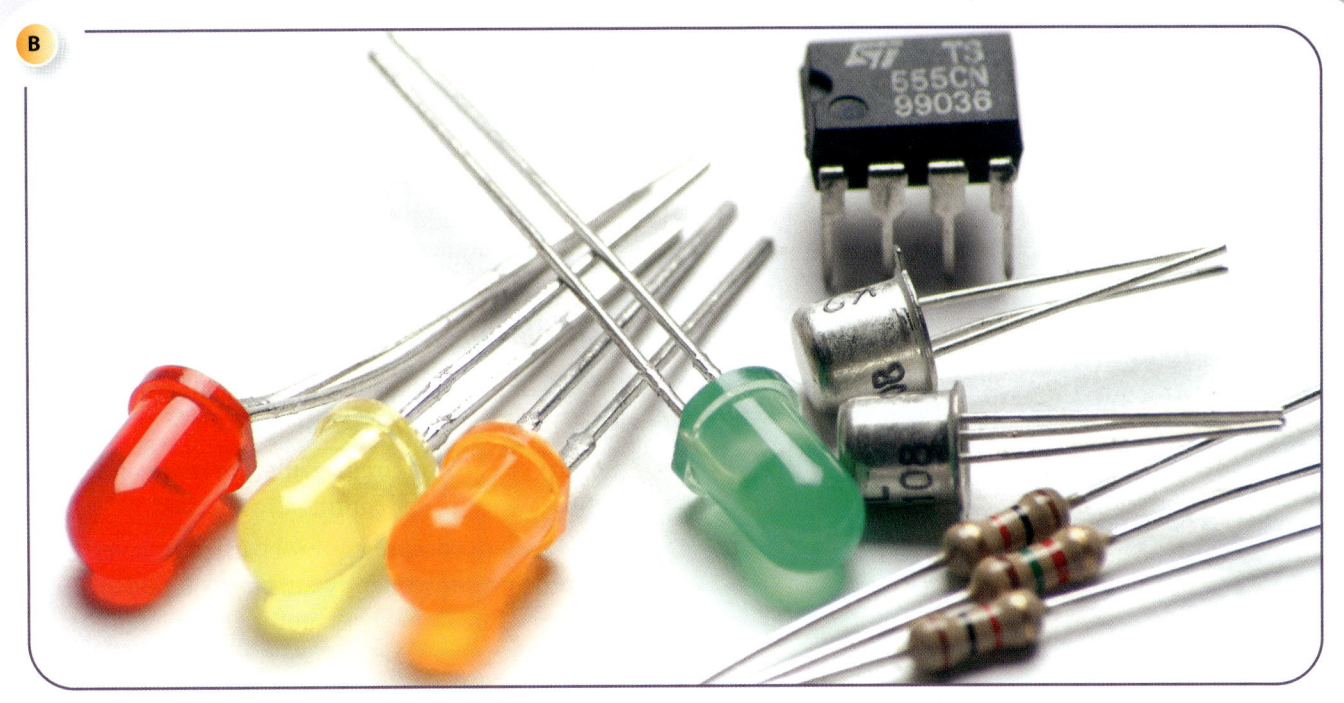

Electrical components

Some of these components will be familiar to you, such as resistors. A capacitor is a device that stores electronic charge. This facility is useful in circuits where different values of small voltages are needed around the circuit for it to work effectively. The arrangement of the components in the radio circuits use capacitors to amplify these small voltages to power the small ear piece so the radio signal can be heard.

There are different design packages that can do this for you, such as PCBwizard and Croc Clips. They may even allow you to test the circuit itself. If you do not have access to a PCB designer, then transfers can be used and as a last resort permanent black pen when drawn on acetate will also work in the photo etch method. Alternatively, it may be that you wish to design your circuit on breadboards, wire wrapping, vero-boards or different modelling boards that allow you to experiment once more with soldering irons and components.

Use this information to help you decide on the best way to develop your radio circuit. You will have to produce a PCB for this project (see page 114).

Alternatively, you may wish to use a readymade circuit board from TEP, Maplins, or RS and simply repackage a new design for the radio. You can be sure that buying a readymade standard circuit board will work and will reduce the likelihood of errors in your work. The use of this standard component will increase the quality of the performance of your product but the way you design and manufacture the final packaging and appearance of the product will affect the aesthetics and its appeal to others.

Remember that many companies use the same standard components from time to time and present them in different ways. This diversity in products provides more choice for potential customers but sometimes such competition would have been at the expense of quality.

Think about it!

How many different ways are there to model your circuit? Which methods are available to you in school? What kind of switch could you use to turn your circuit on and off? How will you mount your circuit, in its case or on its shelf?

Plenary

Producing your own printed circuit boards (PCB's) is a good way of understanding how a circuit works. PCB's are a relatively new technology but electronic circuitry has become so advanced that it is now possible to fit a working circuit on an area the size of a pinhead. What uses do you think this might have?

Testing circuit boards

Objectives

In this lesson you will design, model and test circuit boards.

Key words

breadboard	a plastic device which allows you to use components and integrated circuits without permanent soldering
vero-board	a base for a circuit to be soldered
solder	alloy consisting of tin, lead and flux
counter sink	a 'v' shaped recess for a counter sink screw

Breadboards

A **breadboard** is a plastic device which allows you to use components and integrated circuits without having to solder them permanently together (A). They are quick to use as the user simply pushes in the components in numbered rows and attaches the wires.

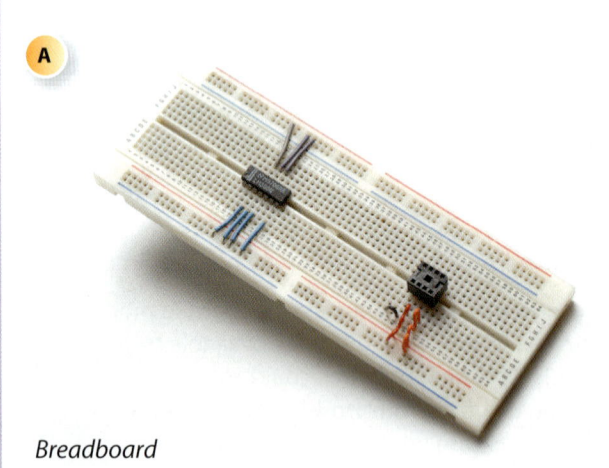

A

Breadboard

Advantages

- You are able to test components and change them with ease.
- It is a cost effective method as you can re-use the components and board after a circuit has been tested.
- At any one time there is only one stage that the designer has to remove or check should things go wrong.
- It is much safer and cleaner as no solder is involved. In addition, you do not risk damaging sensitive components with the heat from the iron.

Disadvantages

- The components can sometimes fall out or are easily disturbed.
- Short circuits or circuit faults are more of a risk if the board is not continually checked.
- It is easy to confuse a breadboard with a **vero-board** and subsequently attach a component leg into the same 'track' as another component, thus short circuiting the device.

Vero-boards, matrix boards or strip boards

These are resin-bonded materials with pre-drilled holes throughout and copper tracks on one side alone (B). Components are soldered onto one side with the legs entering through the holes. The track is then scrapped off where it is not wanted and the circuit can be built bit by bit and acts as a more permanent mock up. However, it can also be used successfully to **solder** up smaller similar circuits.

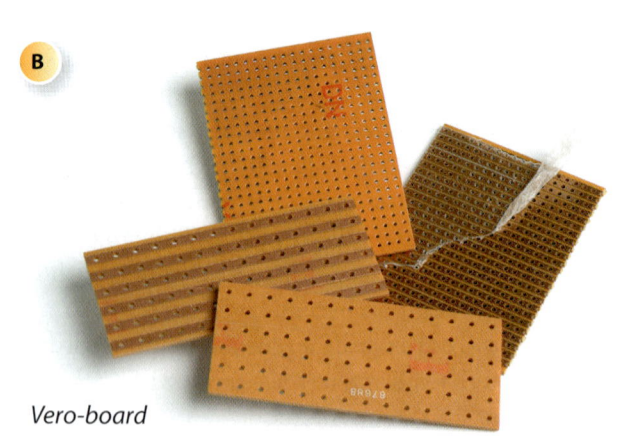

B

Vero-board

Advantages

- The holes for the components are pre-drilled.
- The copper track is run in strips and this can simplify the planning of the circuit.
- It is cheaper than producing a PCB.
- It can be easily shaped by snapping it along the pre-drilled holes.

Disadvantages

- When using a craft knife, hand-held **counter sinks** or drill bits to 'break' away the unwanted copper track, it is easy to snap away other parts of the board that may be needed later.
- Solder can join between two tracks.
- Joins too close together can sometimes unsolder when more components are added and the phenomenon of a 'dry' joint occurs.

FPT Experimenting with vero–boards/PCB and copper wire

See how long it takes for you and a partner to assemble a simple circuit using an LED, a resistor and a power source (battery).

For each of the methods, what issues are involved and what do they suggest about their suitability for a bigger project such as a radio circuit?

Circuit type	Good points	Bad points	Issues and thoughts arising
PCB			
VERO BOARD			
COPPER WIRE			

Wire wrapping

This is a simplified version of both the breadboard and the vero-board. A piece of cardboard or plastic board, approx 2mm thick, is used. Holes are punched into the board using a drawing pin. The legs of the components are then pushed through and wire used on the underside to join up the legs and act as tracks.

Advantages

- Sometimes the circuit can be drawn on the paper to start with to aid construction. This is good practice in advance of breadboarding.
- It is more permanent than breadboarding and there is less chance of components falling out.
- It is relatively low cost as only the components are needed; no soldering is required.

Disadvantages

- The wires can easily come off, especially if more than one is used from a component leg.
- Integrated circuits (IC) are very difficult to manipulate as the legs are short and close together.

Think about it!

At what point in the design process would it be a good idea to use the breadboard or the wire wrapping technique? What reasons can you give for your answer? Why would it be a bad idea to put your circuit together on vero-board first? Can you remember what soft solder is made from?

Plenary

Perfect Planning Prevents Poor Performance! Remember this when you are designing or putting together your circuit.

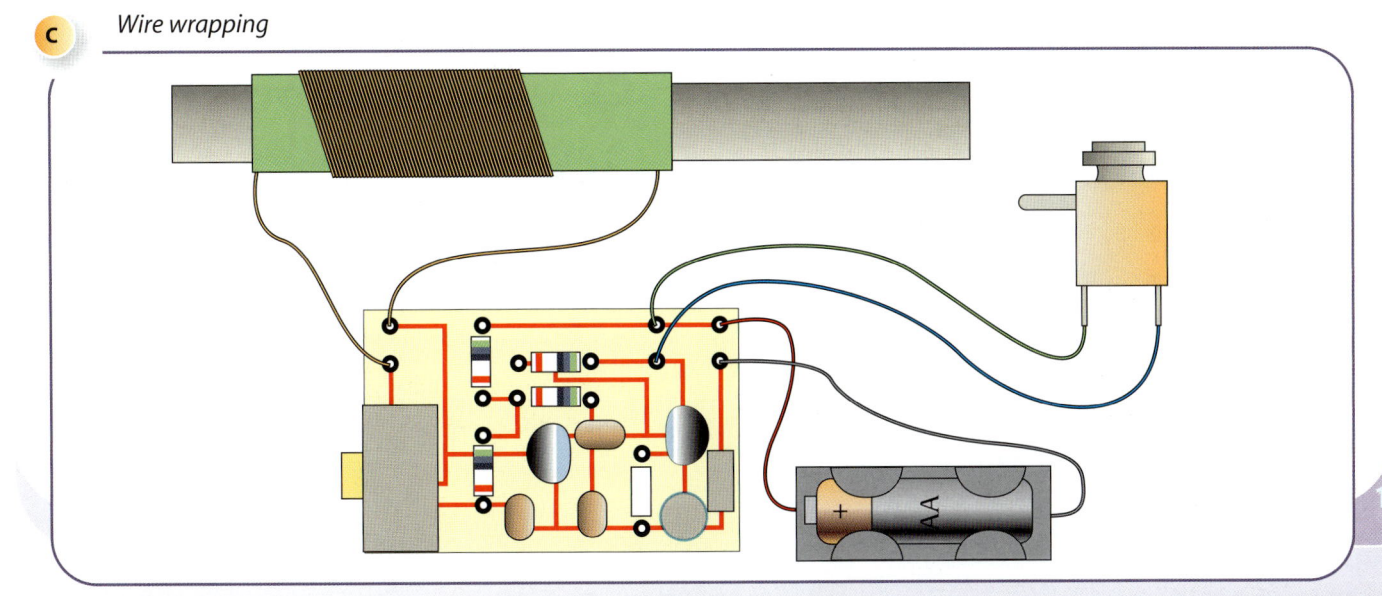

C *Wire wrapping*

Using control for electronic monitoring

Printed circuit boards

Objectives

In this lesson you will:

- design, model and test simple circuit boards
- design printed circuit board masks and use them to make PCBs (if appropriate).

Key words

miniaturization	making a small copy or representation of a larger object
photo etch	part of the process in making a PCB
micro processor	a condensed electronic system found in a computer chip that deals with many differing inputs and outputs collectively

What is a printed circuit board?

A printed circuit board has circuit tracks which are permanently etched onto a plastic board and components can be soldered into position (A). Both components and tracks can be etched onto both layers. There is a PCB to be found within nearly all-electronic devices, such as a toaster, a radio, television, telephone, computer, watches, alarm systems even musical birthday cards contain a small version of a PCB.

Some electronic products make use of the PCB as part of its decoration. Seeing inside the component sometimes makes people feel more comfortable with the device as they can see what is going on inside it.

Printed circuit boards are used as a final prototype when the designer is confident that the circuit he or she has designed will work time after time. From the PCB, further developments can be made so that the circuit can be reduced even further. Parts of the circuit can sometimes be made into an integrated circuit. The net effect of this process is **miniaturization**. This allows large circuits to be developed and tested at different stages so that, finally, the products at the end of the process are small, efficient and inexpensive to produce. The power they consume is less and therefore battery life can be extended.

A

Track side

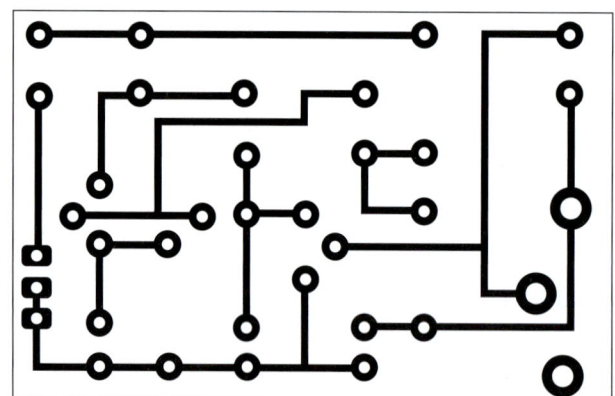

Transparent view

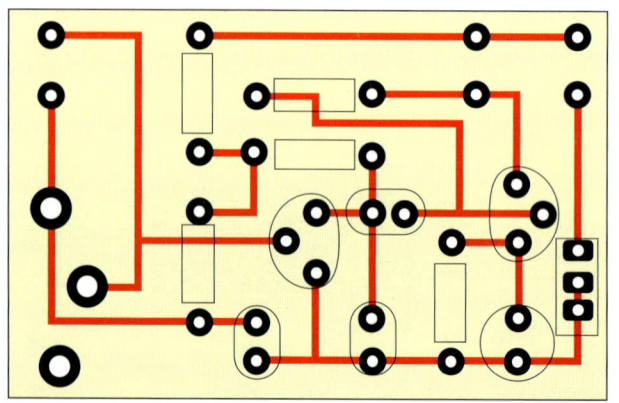

Etching

The **photo etch** method allows you to produce a PCB at school. Here, the circuit tracks are designed as if you are looking down through the board from above. This is printed off actual size on clear acetate. This sheet is then laid upon the plastic board. The plastic board is a laminated board made of plastic, a layer of copper, a light photosensitive layer and a protective layer of self-adhesive peel-off plastic. The final layer prevents natural light falling on the light sensitive surface, but is removed when the acetate is ready to be positioned. The board is then exposed to ultraviolet light. This process acts very much like a photograph. The light cannot penetrate the black ink of the track lines on the acetate and so leaves an outline of the tracks which is later etched away to reveal the copper tracks.

Using CAD and CAM

There are a range of programmes that allow you to make the process easier and some CAD/ CAM packages that may even produce circuit boards by scratching away excess copper. Whatever process is used, the end result is the same – a useable, ready to solder board.

To help your design brief it is useful to consider what the final outcome will look like.

Design six different radio fronts for six different radio stations. These can be based around:

- the station name
- the station Frequency on the FM / AM dial
- the station genre and what sort of music / entertainment of information you would find on it.

Below is a bill of materials. Use this as a format for your own radio material requests. As you plan out the radio, you can propose costing and work out how much you would have to sell it for in order to make a marketable product and profit for more investment in the future.

Materials required	
Cost of item	
Units required	
Dimensions of materials	
Cost of materials	
Tools needed	
Components	
Solder	
PCB materials	
Cost of labour	
Total outgoings	

The impact of PCB technology cannot be over stated. It developed in the early 1950's and led to a massive acceleration in the design and manufacture of electronic goods. Products became faster, more reliable, cheaper and plentiful. To this day **microprocessors** are becoming smaller and smaller. The smaller they are, the faster they can operate and the more computers can do as they handle more information. PCB's hold the components securely in nearly all electronic goods.

Think about it!

Planning the construction of your radio is essential. A well thought out plan will result in a high quality product and a stress free experience. Use the flow chart symbols (see page 102–3) to plan the construction of your radio from collecting the parts to the final assembly.

Tip… Bullet-point each stage first with a pencil and then incorporate the flow chart symbols.

Plenary

When working out labour costs be realistic. If this product were being made by a big multi national company how many different people would be involved in its production. How many products would have to sell to cover their wages? More than you can count on your fingers and toes!

Design and make a radio

Objectives

In this lesson you will:
- design a radio using a range of technologies, including computer control
- ensure your radio meets a specific purpose and the needs of the intended user.

Key words

circuit	an unbroken flow of electrical current
CAD	Computer Aided Design
CAM	Computer Aided Manufacturer
aesthetics	how we respond to the visual appearance of a product

DMA Design and make a radio

The design brief

To design and manufacture an AM radio.

This radio needs to be produced within the bill of materials your teacher will demonstrate and explain. An example of the model used by designers is shown in diagram A.

The casing of the radio can be based on a design style from the twentieth century. By combining two or three different materials in interesting ways and cutting them to different shapes, you will be able to create an imaginative and eye-catching product without the need to think of complicated ideas. Alternatively, you could chose one of the following design briefs on these pages.

Design specification

- The design must be original
- You must use two different materials
- It must have a high quality of finish
- It must be safe to use
- It must take the end users interests into account
- It must house the **circuit** and a 9volt battery and an on/off switch

A

Basic model radio

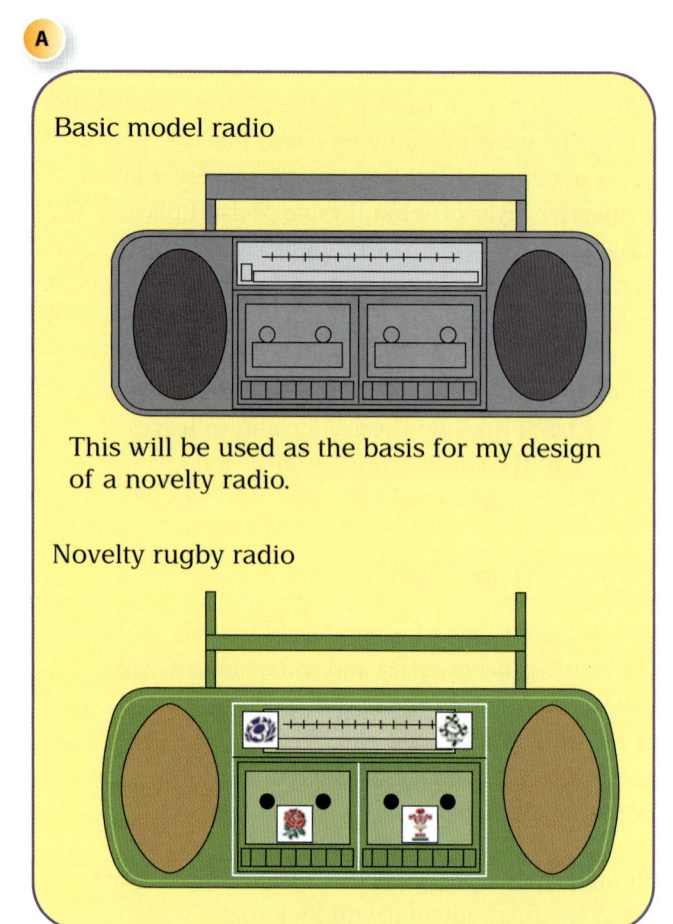

This will be used as the basis for my design of a novelty radio.

Novelty rugby radio

Think about it!

1. Ask people what music they like listening to, who their favourite bands and pop stars are and so on. Design the front of the radio to suit their taste.
2. Design a poster for a new radio station aimed at your subjects' music tastes.

You need to consider many things when designing this radio and developing your ideas. Having mindmapped your ideas and sketched possible designs for the outside casing of your work, you need to choose an idea based on how well you think you can manipulate materials. For example, consider whether you going to vacuum form a casing, or are going to cut different pieces of acrylic or MDF either by hand or using a **CAD/CAM** programme (remember flat sheets can often slot together into 3D forms).

The plan of your work will depend on your bill of materials and what aspect needs to come first. For example, are you going to make the circuit first and then build the body, or are you going to build the body and then insert the circuit?

Ask other people how well you are doing and get their opinions of your design ideas and manufacturing. This process is part of Quality Assurance and if followed correctly, the final outcome will be of a high standard.

Design brief ideas

Bicycle! Bicycle!

A mountain bike manufacturer wishes to add an AM radio as a standard extra for bikers to listen to when they rest or reach their destinations. They should be able to receive music, weather and travel information. The design exterior must reflect mountain biking as an activity and be able to attach and detach easily but without being knocked off.

Driven by you

As a complementary gift, a car showroom wishes to give away radios that are shaped as products that are associated with motoring. Examples of these include dashboard dials, gear sticks, wing mirrors, bumpers and tyres.

Lets go surfing!

A radio for surfers needs to be mounted high up away from the sand on the beach. It should be able to catch weather reports and coastguard information. It might be styled with a surf or sail theme.

Romantic radio

For late night listeners, a radio could be designed with love as its theme. This can be targeted to go on sale for Valentines Day, anniversaries and birthdays.

All around the world

For the globetrotting individual or international businessman, a travel radio which will pick up local stations. This radio could be based on a country, flag or language for its design.

We are the champions!

Design a radio for supporters of a team or an individual sportsman that shows the colours and emblems of the sport. The radio could have the appearance of a trophy or a ball or part of the sporting equipment used.

B

Think about it!

1 **LIT** Firstly, research the market and seek the opinions of people who you would expect to use your radio.

2 **D** Draw up a detailed design specification for your radio. Remember to include the following:
- **aesthetics**
- technical function
- usability
- reliability
- maintenance
- quality
- health and safety.

Plenary

If all of these radios were to be produced by the same company as a new product range what could the company do to each design and each product so that the consumer can see that they are all from the same company?

Using control for electronic monitoring

Designing your radio

Objectives
In this lesson you will design a user interface for your radio, which suits its purpose and intended user.

Key words
modelling	3D experiments that designers use to help them design
proposal	put forward an idea or suggestion

Developing your ideas

Use the following research suggestions to help develop your ideas further:

- Origins of radio: its discovery and evolution, where radios were first used, famous case studies and names, such as electromagnetic spectrum.
- Design history of the radio: streaming from the 1950s, Bakelite radio, Bush, Robert's radio, Trevor Bayliss and the wind-up radio.

- Uses: where are radios used today and what are they used for? What information is transmitted via radios?
- Radio stations and programmes: how many radio stations can you find and what sort of audience are they aimed at? Where and when can you listen to current affairs, political programmes, classical music, jazz, pop music, talk shows, or lifestyle programmes?
- Free radio: where and when might free radios be delivered to people, and what would be the benefits or drawbacks of such a scheme? Think about disaster areas, rock festivals, local island radio, flying doctors, school or hospital radio.

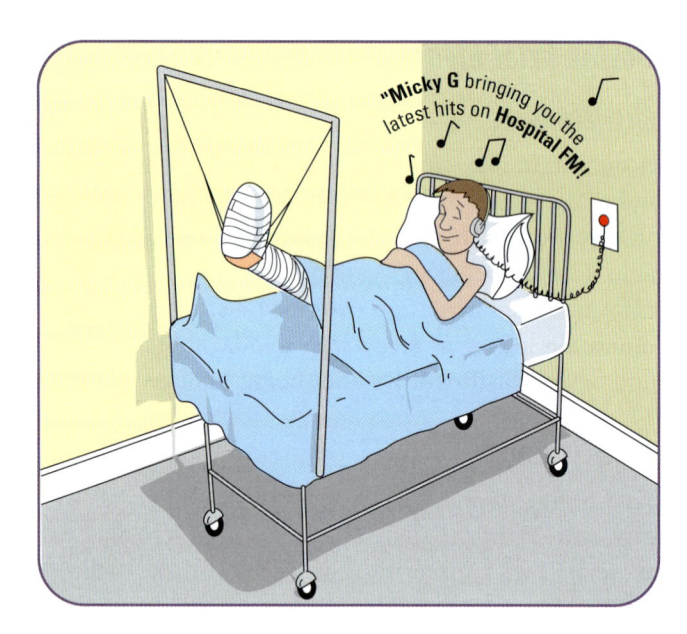

- Electronic feedback: what electronic systems in the home use electronic feedback and what form does it take?
- Radio on the move: where and for whom?

Designing your radio case

Now that you have created your radio it is time to design the radio case. Even if the circuit works perfectly it will all be for nothing if the quality of the case or surround is of a low standard. You need to focus your ideas on the needs of your end user first. Who are you making the product for? What are their likes and dislikes? What are their favourite colours and music tastes? Where they will put the radio? Produce a questionnaire to find out this information and then put it onto a mood board.

You will need to investigate and choose a material to use for the construction of your case or platform. You may prefer to choose a material that you are confident with or choose a material that is suggested by your end user. Test the material before you begin to make the radio. Can it be drilled without it falling apart or shattering? Can you glue things to it? Can you paint or add colour to it? How much will it cost? Does the school have any or do you have to get it from an outside source?

A

Different types of radio listening appeals to different types of people

When you have finalised your design idea model it using card and then show it to the end user. **Modelling** your idea could save time and money because this is a chance to spot any design faults, which can then be easily rectified.

Once all the problems have been ironed out at the modelling stage assembly can begin. You can use the plan you produced on page 117 or produce a new one for this part of production if you have not already done so. Think about what tools and materials you will need. Make a cutting list (a list of all of the pieces of material you will need and their sizes) and check it through with your teacher to ensure that all the materials and components are available. If possible involve the end user at every stage so that you can solve problems as they occur rather than leaving it until the end of the project when things are harder to fix.

Finally when you have completed your product reflect on what you have achieved to evaluate your product.

Think about it!

Ask yourself these questions.
1. What have I learnt during this project?
2. What went wrong and how did I rectify the problem?
3. What does my end-user think of the product?
4. What part did I enjoy most?
5. If I could do the project again what would I change and why?
6. If the product were to be produced in greater numbers how could this be done?
7. How long did it take me to produce it?
8. How could I reduce this time if I did this project again?

Think about it!

1. **D** Carry out some modelling to explore and test your thinking, before deciding on a final **proposal**. Think carefully about how the system will communicate with the user and how the user will communicate with the system.
2. **ABC** Produce a simple user guide that describes:
   a) what the product does
   b) how it should be used
   c) how it should be cared for and maintained.

Plenary

When producing a set of instructions for a product you have designed it is important to realise that this will be the first time the end user has come into contact with your product. You must therefore make your instruction as simple as possible. Using pictures and annotated sketches will help with this process.

UNIT 12 — Moving on to Key Stage 4

Getting ready for Key Stage 4

Objectives

In this lesson you will:
- learn to be critical of yourself and to be able to identify your strengths and weaknesses
- set yourself targets for the future.

Key words

evaluate	thinking about why and how products are designed and made and how they function
target	something that is aimed for, a challenge

During Key Stage 3 you have been developing your skills in designing, making and **evaluating** (justifying and learning to review). You have also been developing your skills in communicating. You have a good idea of the activities you prefer to work on, and the ones that you learned the most from. You will know what your strengths and weaknesses are, and what you found easy or difficult. Are you good at giving reasons for your design decisions?

What you have to do now is to reflect on your own performance, consider how you have progressed and set yourself some real **targets** to work towards.

You need to measure and record exactly what you know, understand and can do.

By thinking hard and recording honestly, you will be able to see where you need to focus your efforts over the next two years. You need to set your aims high and work hard to reach the highest possible level of attainment.

Targets – taking control of your attainment

Setting yourself a target is the first step to improving your attainment. Once you have established what you find difficult, you can start to consider what you need to do to get better. This is the most important part. Of course, it goes without saying that once you have set yourself targets, they must be worked on if you are to get better at Design and Technology.

Think about it!

1. Draw a table similar to table A.
   a) **TS** Think about your own performance (your subject knowledge, designing skills, making skills, and your ability to **evaluate** and communicate).
   b) Complete the table.
   c) Look closely at exactly what you can do and make a list of these things.
   d) Look at where you are not performing as well. Make a list of these areas too.
   e) Set yourself targets to improve these areas and state how you intend to achieve this.

2. From the table you have completed on your performance, identify a maximum of five areas you need to work on.
   a) For each area, identify what exactly you are going to do to improve the skill.
   b) Draw a table like the one below to help you record your targets.

Skills area to improve	How to improve it

   c) Record your targets, remembering that you need to state how you intend to achieve them. You can make a difference to your own performance.

Plenary

Reflecting on your own strengths and weaknesses and setting yourself targets based on this information are a good ways to improve your attainment levels.

Moving on to Key Stage 4

Copy and complete the table, place a tick in the correct column.

A

Area for development	Can do	Can do well	Need to improve
THE DESIGN PROCESS			
Designing skills			
Clarifying the task			
• Understanding the task			
• Interpreting the task			
• Recording the design considerations			
Generating ideas			
• Evolving ideas, adapting and adjusting ideas			
• Diversifying ideas, wide range of possible ideas			
• Proposing design possibilities			
Developing ideas			
• Modelling design possibilities			
• Refining design ideas			
• Stating how the product could be made			
• Techniques and processes to be used			
Communicating intentions			
• Verbally			
• Graphically-technical, visual and pictorial			
• Modelling			
Producing quality products			
Planning			
• Materials needed			
• Equipment required			
• Making sequence time plan			
Working with materials			
• Selecting, measuring, marking out			
• Cutting, shaping, joining fabrics,			
Health and safety issues			
• Using tools and equipment safely			
• Recognizing hazards			
Evaluating skills – reviewing processes and products			
• During designing and making			
• After designing and making			
Learning methods – the way you learn best			
Focused Practical Tasks			
• Design skills			
• Making skills			
Product Analysis			
• Looking at existing products			
Designing and making projects			
• Independent work			
• Team work			

Glossary

aesthetics how we respond to the visual appearance of a product

aluminium a light silver coloured metal

annotating notes on a design that explain the materials used and how it will work

anthropometric study of the measurments of the human body

aperture a gap or shape cut within material

assets useful or valuable items such as materials

batch production a method of production where a number of parts are all made at once by several different people

bell crank change the direction of a force around a corner

bevel gears toothed gears that are set at an angle

bi-colour LED a red and green LED with two leads, only one LED can be on at any time

breadboard a plastic device which allows you to use components and integrated circuits without permanent soldering

buzzers a component that vibrates when a current passes through

cams objects that sit on a crank and bring about a change in motion

circuit an unbroken flow of electrical current

closed question a question with only a limited number of possible answers

compression a squashing force

CAD Computer Aided Design

CAM Computer Aided Manufacture

conductive a material that can carry electricity or heat

coniferous trees that do not lose their leaves in winter

consumer a person who buys products

control system a series of commands to obtain a desired outcome

correflute corrugated plastic sheeting

corrugated card two sheets of cards sandwiching a corrugated core

counter sink a 'v' shaped recess for a counter sink screw

crank follower a supporting leg of a cam that follows a cam when it is rotated

deciduous trees that lose their leaves in winter

dip coating a process of coating metal with plastic

dry joint a joint that is not permanently fixed together

ductile a material that is able to be shaped and moulded

eccentric cams off-centered wheels on a shaft

effort amount of force required to lift something

electrical components small devices that transfer electric current into other forms of energy or change electric current flow

endorse to give approval of a product

enduring long lasting

equipment the tools used to make the materials into products

evaluate thinking about why and how products are designed and made and how they function

Exertris product name: interactive exercise system

ferrous a material that contains iron

finish to put a final coating on material

flow chart a chart using symbols to show the sequence of a process

foam board foam sandwiched between card

force something that makes an object move

fulcrum pivot point

gears meshing wheels with teeth that link together to transfer motion

glass paper a paper coated in glass particles used to smooth wood

hardwood wood from deciduous trees

hazard an event that could cause harm to someone

hydraulic controlling systems by the use of fluids

input what is done at the beginning of a process

insulator a material that blocks electricity or heat

isometric a way of drawing objects in three dimensions

jig a device manufactured to assist designers and makers to maintain accuracy when repeating the same operation time and again

just-in-time (JIT) production stock control in industry which involves designing and making in response to demands

kiln a large oven or furnace for drying

lacquered a protective coating applied with a brush or aerosol

laminated coating of thin layers

lay planning the plan of where to lay out jigs and templates to use the least amount of material and do the least cutting

lever a mechanism that lifts, pulls apart or squashes forces

Light Emitting Diodes (LEDs) a small bulb used in an electric circuit

linear movement in one direction only

linkage used to control movement and change the direction of force

lustrous when an object has a shiny or reflective surface

man-made board materials such as plywood or MDF

market research the method of finding out what people like and need in a product

materials the items different products are made from

mechanical advantage allows a user to move a large load without needing a large force

MDF man made fibre

micro-controllers small computers which control light, sound, movement and so on

microprocessor a condensed electronic system found in a computer chip that deals with many differing inputs and outputs collectively

miniaturization making a small copy or representation of a larger object

modelling 3D experiments that designers use to help them design

mood board a starting point for a design idea, a collection of images and ideas that convey a mood or reaction - sometimes known as a mindmapping page

mounting board thick card

non-corrosive a material that will not rust

objectively looking at something without influence of personal feelings or opinions

Ohms law the method used to calculate resistance

one-off production a product required as a single item

open-ended question a question with many possible answers and responses

oscillating movement back and forth along an arc

output what happens at the end of a process

oxides a compound of oxygens

oxidization when a metal reacts with the oxygen in the air

PDD product design company: product innovation consultants

photo etch part of the process in making a PCB

pictorial flow chart a flow chart using very few words

pilot hole a small hole used to guide a screw

pivot point around which an object turns

planish to smooth, flatten or finish metal

pneumatic system control movements by the use of compressed air

point-of-sale display (POSD) a device to promote new products

printed circuit board (PCB) a circuit formed by printing or soldering the circuit onto a surface instead of using wires

product lifecycle the changing sales of a product during its time on the market

proposal put forward an idea or suggestion

prototype a model or product which has been made to be tested or trialled before being put into full production

pulleys a series of wheels connected by ropes or belts and used to transfer or lift loads with little effort

PVA glue water based adhesive

PVC Poly Vinyl Chloride a type of plastic that comes in hard or soft varieties

quality control checking that quality has not dropped during manufacture

reciprocating movement backwards and forwards in a straight line

rendering adding colour, form or texture to a drawn or made object

resin a solid or liquid compound used in plastics

resistance materials that resist electric current and turn it into heat

resistor an electrical component to limit the flow of current in a circuit

risk the likelihood that a hazard will occur

rotary circular movement

signal a wave of sound that transmits information

smart materials materials that are able to react to the user or the environment such as changes in temperature, moisture, pH or electrical and magnetic fields

soft jaws jaws of a vice that will not damage the surface of a material

softwood wood from coniferous trees

solder alloy consisting of tin, lead and flux

specification a list of criteria that a new design must meet

standardized component a common item that is produced in thousands and each one is identical

steel a hard metal

structure the way something is put together

switches a break in the circuit that can be controlled safely

target something that is aimed for, a challenge

template a shape used by designers to draw around and to mark up materials so that the same shape and quality of accuracy are repeated each time

tension a pulling apart force

TEP bug kit a kit to help you create a bug available from TEP

thermoplastic a type of plastic which when resoftend under heat can have its shape changed many times

thermosetting a type of plastic that once set cannot change shape

tolerance the amount of difference that is acceptable between two products that are said to be identical

vacuum forming a process which moulds a thin plastic sheet to form a shape

varnished a glossy finish to a surface

velocity ratio the relationship between input and output in a mechanical system

veneered thin layers of wood, plastic and so on used to cover a surface to improve appearance

vero-board a base for a circuit to be soldered

wood grain the lines made by fibres in wood which all go in one direction

Index

acrylic polishing	59
adhesives	28–9
aesthetics	86, 88–9, 94, 118
alarm circuits	63
aluminium	6, 32–3, 108
animatronic operations	68–9
annotation	16–17, 92
aperture	18, 19
assembly of bug kit	72–3
assets	106
automatic systems	53
batch production	78–9
bi-colour LEDs	70–1
boards	28
see also circuit boards; mind boards	
breadboards	114
bug kit	68–73
CAD (Computer Aided Design)	46, 52–3, 82, 108, 117–18
CAM (Computer Aided Manufacture)	46, 52–3, 82, 108, 117–18
cams	22, 36, 66–7
card (correflute)	28
case studies	50–1, 92–3
ceramics	87
circuit boards	112–17
circuits	110–11
classics	90–1
clips and slots	30–1
closed questions	98
codes, plastic types	41
colour codes, resistors	57
components	
standardized	82
compression	26–7
Computer Aided Design see CAD	
Computer Aided Manufacture see CAM	
computer aided systems	53
consumer choice	96
consumer society	98–9
consumers	96–7
control systems	60–3
correflute card	28
counter sinks	114–15
cranks	66–7
cutting	18, 19
design brief	12
design company	50–1
design specification	12, 14
designing techniques	48–9
detectors, light/darkness	63
developing ideas	17, 51
dip coating	35
displays	20–1, 28–9, 81
dyes	39
efficiency	65
effort	64
electrical components	24–5
electronics	56–7, 68–73, 112–13
enamelling	35
endorsing products	20–1
environment	86–7
equipment	4, 5
etching	116–17
evaluation	16–17, 44–5, 72–3, 122–3
Exertris case study	50–1
ferrous materials	6
files	38–9, 59
finish (lustrous)	34
finishing	38–9, 42–3
fire resistant materials	109
flow charts	102–3
foam board	28
followers	66–7
forces	26–7, 62
forming plastics	40–1
gears	22
glass paper	38–9
glues see adhesives	
grain	38–9
hardwood	8–9, 36
hazards	76–7, 108–9
see also safety	
health & safety	74–5, 76
heat treatment	33
holes	18–19
hydraulic systems	60
ideas	14–15, 17, 51
inputs	60, 61, 62
IQ micro-controllers	69, 70–1
isometric drawing	16
jigs	18, 19, 58–9, 78–81
joints	56
just-in-time production	106–7, 108
Key Stage 4 preparation	122–3
kilns	36, 37
lacquer	74
laminate	74
lay planning	84–5
LEDs see Light Emitting Diodes	

127

levers	64–5
lifecycles, products	104
light detectors	63
Light Emitting Diodes (LEDs)	24, 25, 56–7, 70–1
linear movement	20–1
linkages	22, 23, 66–7
loss and profit	104–5
lustrous finish	34
man-made woods	37
see also MDF	
manufacture see production	
market research	48–9, 98–9
marketing	105
materials	4, 5, 28–9, 86–7, 109
MDF (Medium Density Fibreboard)	8–9, 28, 37, 74–5
mechanical advantage	64–5
mechanisms	22–3
media storage unit	84–5
Medium Density Fibreboard see MDF	
metals	6–7, 32–3
micro-controllers	68, 70–1
mind mapping	48–9
miniaturization	116
modelling	48, 92–3, 120
mood boards	14
objectivity	44–5
Ohms Law	56
one-off production	54–5, 107
open-ended questions	98
oscillating movement	20–1
outputs	60, 61, 62
oxides	34, 56
paint	34, 39, 87
PCBs see printed circuit boards	
pencils	82–3
pilot holes	18–19
planishing	32, 35
planning	50–1, 84–5
plastics	10–11, 35, 40–3
plating	34–5
plywood	19
pneumatic systems	60
point-of-sale displays (POSDs)	20–1, 28–9, 30–1
polishing acrylics	59
POSDs see point-of-sale displays	
power sources	24–5, 56
printed circuit boards (PCBs)	112–13, 116–17
product analysis	5, 14, 88–9
product concept models	92–3
product lifecycles	104
production	74–5, 78–9, 89, 104–7
profit and loss	104–5
programming	70–1
proposals	120
prototypes	54–5, 92
pulleys	22, 23
PVA glue	28–9
PVC (Poly Vinyl Chloride)	10–11

quality	100–1
questionnaires	98
radios	110–11, 118–21
razors	88–9, 91, 94–5
reciprocating	20–1
rendering	16–17
researching ideas	51
resin	37, 41, 42–3
resistance	24–5, 56–7
risk	76–7, 108
rotary movement	20–1
safety	40–1, 74–5
seasoning wood	37
security systems	62–3
shape memory alloys	87
shaping	18, 19, 38
signals	110–11
sketching	16
slots and clips	30–1
smart materials	86–7, 92–3
soft jaws	18–19
softwood	8–9, 36
soldering	56–7, 113–15
specification	12–13, 46–7
staining wood	39
standardized components	82
steel	6, 32
structure	26–7, 88
surveys	98
switches	57
targets	122–3
templates	58–9, 78–81
tension	26–7
thermo ceramics	87
thermoplastics	10–11
thermosetting plastics	10–11
tolerance	100–1
vacuum forming	40–1
varnish	39, 74
vehicle guidance	53
velocity ratio	64, 65
veneer	74
vero-boards	114
wire wrapping	115
wood	8–9, 36–7, 38–9